The Productive Small Garden

The Productive
Small Garden

SUE PHILLIPS

PELHAM BOOKS
STEPHEN GREENE PRESS

PELHAM BOOKS/STEPHEN GREENE PRESS

Published by the Penguin Group
27 Wrights Lane, London W8 5TZ, England
Viking Penguin Inc., 40 West 23rd Street, New York, New York 10010, USA
The Stephen Greene Press, 15 Muzzey Street, Lexington, Massachusetts 02173, USA
Penguin Books Australia Ltd, Ringwood, Victoria, Australia
Penguin Books Canada Ltd, 2801 John Street, Markham, Ontario, Canada L3R 1B4
Penguin Books (NZ) Ltd, 182–190 Wairau Road, Auckland 10, New Zealand

Penguin Books Ltd, Registered Offices: Harmondsworth, Middlesex, England

First published 1989

Made and printed in Great Britain by
Butler and Tanner Ltd, Frome, Somerset

Typeset by Wilmaset, Birkenhead, Wirral

ISBN 0–7207–1867–8

A CIP catalogue record for this book is available
from the British Library

Contents

Photo Credits

The black and white photographs are reproduced by permission of the author and the colour photographs by permission of the author and Michael Warren.

Introduction

Gardens are shrinking; each year the amount of garden space allocated to new houses seems to get less. And gardening itself is changing. Nowadays people want much more from their gardens – increasingly we want them to be more fashionable, ornamental, recreational, stylish and individual than ever before. The plants we put in gardens are changing, too; compact and heavy yielding fruit and vegetables, dwarfer bedding plants and shorter perennials that our grandfathers would hardly recognise; even the way we do things is different – new gardening ideas, techniques and equipment appear on our TV screens and in magazines regularly. Gardens don't even look the same. Now, creative planting styles are all the rage. Anything is possible – you can have a garden based on paving, wild flowers, pools, old-fashioned cottage-garden flowers, 'low-maintenance' shrubs and ground-cover plants, or a bit of everything – fruit, flowers and vegetables – for the whole family to enjoy.

With so many changes going on in the gardening world, it can be hard to keep up. This book demonstrates the best of the new – and the newly revived old – techniques, products, plants, ideas and planting schemes that will help make your small garden more productive; a facility to be enjoyed to the full – whether you garden for edible crops, as a creative outlet or just for relaxation in pleasant surroundings.

Its aim, quite simply, is to help you get more out of a small garden, while at the same time perhaps putting less into it!

Chapter 1

Vegetables

Really fresh home-grown vegetables are a luxury everyone can enjoy, because nowadays there is room to grow at least a few crops in even the smallest of gardens – particularly if you don't mind setting aside some of the traditional growing methods and trying something a bit different. In fact, scientists who work on improving the productivity of commercial vegetable crops reckon that gardeners at home could get up to 40 per cent more vegetables from the same space, just by putting a few of their new discoveries – and a few half-forgotten old ones – into practice.

To improve productivity from a small plot, there are two things to look at: what you grow, and how you grow it. In a really tiny garden it is a complete waste of space to grow things that are cheap in the shops, such as maincrop potatoes and onions. It is much better, therefore, to grow those that give the biggest return in terms of culinary or monetary value – for instance, crops that taste best only when they are picked and eaten the same day, such as spinach, snap peas and lettuce, often way past their best when you buy them; or the slightly unusual 'gourmet' vegetables that are difficult to get in the shops, such as golden courgettes, kohl rabi or purple French beans. Multi-purpose crops can give you two vegetables from the space of one, for example Hamburg parsley (which produces parsley leaves above ground, and a root like parsnip below); and there are some vegetables that are always terribly expensive to buy, such as asparagus or globe artichokes. Good value, too, are enormously productive crops like runner beans, or those which give a fast turnover like radish. Plus, of course, you can include any vegetable you particularly like growing, giant pumpkins perhaps, because gardens are, after all, supposed to be about enjoying yourself too.

As for the actual growing techniques you use, the trick here is to make the most, not just of the space available, but also of the

1

entire growing season. You can do this by using a combination of new varieties – compact, fast-maturing kinds, like Pixie cabbage; vegetables that occupy the ground when it is normally empty, like over-wintering onions; new intensive-growing techniques, such as deep beds; and new products, like floating cloches that help to extend the growing season – all of which make it possible to pack more into a small space, and get much more out of it. Best of all, these methods very often involve much less effort than traditional vegetable growing. And even if you don't have room for a separate vegetable garden, many varieties are pretty enough to grow in a border alongside the flowers. Plenty more can be grown in growing bags or pots on what are otherwise unproductive areas of paving. So let's look in detail at what you can do to get more vegetables from a small space.

Vegetable Plant Production

Raising Plants under Glass

In spring, early sown outdoor vegetables take a long time to grow as the soil is so cold. But if you have a greenhouse or cold frame, you can speed things up by sowing your early crops in trays and raising them under glass. This way, you can sow several weeks earlier than usual, and have young plants ready to put in at about the same time as you would normally be sowing outside. By gaining a head start in this way, your early crops will then be really early and you will be eating them while they are still expensive to buy in the shops. But there is another advantage in sowing under glass. By raising *all* your young plants under glass, not just the early ones, you can get the next batch started in the greenhouse while the first crop is still growing in the garden. As soon as you clear one crop, the next plants are ready to go in. And because no time is wasted waiting for seed to germinate, the ground is never empty, and you can get an extra crop, or even two, from the plot over the course of a season.

Multi-seeding

The normal way of raising vegetable plants under glass is to sow the seeds in pots, prick the seedlings out, and grow them on in the greenhouse until they are ready for planting. But now there is an

2

even better way – a new technique known as multi-seeding. This is a very intensive way of growing young vegetable plants, which saves a lot of the effort, materials and space normally needed – not to mention cost. The idea is that you grow the plants in pots, but instead of growing one young plant in each, you grow several all together. So, you make a big saving on pots and compost for a start. The seeds are sown straight into pots, and the seedlings thinned out to leave two to five of the strongest (depending on the kind of vegetable plant you are growing), so there is no pricking out to do – a big saving in time. The young plants are grown on as usual, and when they are big enough the whole potful is planted out just as it is – in a clump, without splitting it up. You will need to space the 'clumps' of plants at rather wider spacings than usual, but this is an advantage, as wider spacing makes for easier weeding – you are less likely to 'nick' plants with the hoe.

Multi-seeding can be used to raise all the plants you would normally grow in trays and prick out – like cabbage, lettuce, sprouts, leeks, onions, herbs and so on. It can also be used for crops you would usually sow individually in pots, such as sweetcorn, marrows, courgettes, French beans, etc. But multi-seeding can also be used for a lot of crops you would normally never try to prick out or transplant – root vegetables such as beetroot, carrots and turnips (round- or stump-rooted varieties only are suitable), and things like spring onions, or dill. This is only possible because the seeds are sown straight into a pot and are grown on and planted without any root disturbance whatsoever. But the thing that is most surprising about multi-seeding is the way onions, beetroot, carrots and turnips, don't end up square – which, grown so close together in clumps, you would expect them to do. Somehow the plants jostle for space, and produce good-sized crops of perfect-shaped roots, the same as usual.

So if you fancy giving multi-seeding a try, here's what to do.

Use any kind of small individual pots measuring about 1–2 ins (25–50 mm) across – peat are best for multi-seeding but you could also use plastic, or the kind of polystyrene trays that are divided up into small squares. Fill them with any good brand of seed compost, and sow a small pinch of seed into the centre of each. (Sow about two or three times as many seeds as you want plants.) Barely cover the seed with a little more compost, and water well. Stand the pots on a bench in the greenhouse, or for even faster results, put them in an electrically heated propagator until the seeds just start to come up. Then take them out, and grow them on the bench as usual, keeping them shaded from bright sunlight. You will probably find that multi-seeded plants need more water than usual while they are under glass, as there are more plants in each pot. When the seedlings are big enough, thin to leave only the strongest (see chart). They are ready for planting as soon as the pot fills with roots. You can tell when this is by lifting the pots occasionally to see if roots are beginning to appear through the drainage holes. It is even easier if you use peat pots, as the roots actually start growing out through the sides of the pots. It is specially important to plant root crops at this stage, or they may 'fang' later. To plant, knock the plants carefully out of their plastic pots or polystyrene trays; but those grown in peat pots are planted 'pot and all'. Whichever you use, avoid breaking up the ball of roots at all; plant the clump just as it is. Plant into well-prepared ground, at the spacing shown in the chart opposite:

SOWING OUTDOORS

Supposing you do not own a greenhouse or cold frame, and have to sow your vegetable seeds in the open? There is still a lot you can do to boost productivity.

Seed Viability

The most important thing is to make sure you get one hundred per cent of the potential crop from your plot – every space filled with vegetables – which means no empty gaps where the seeds didn't come up. There are several techniques that help here, but whichever you follow, it always makes sense to use fresh (i.e. this year's) seed. Although some kinds of vegetable seed will come up after they have been kept several years, with most, the percentage that germinate will drop very quickly – so if you have to sow old seed, sow it thickly. Some seeds, such as parsnip, salsify and Hamburg parsley, rarely come up after the year that you buy them, so they are not worth keeping.

Lining Seed Drills

If you garden on less than perfect soil, a very simple technique that helps outdoor seed germination is to line your seed drills with ½ in. (12 mm) of peat or vermiculite before sowing. Just use a

VEGETABLE	NO. PER POT	PLANTING DISTANCE	NOTES
BEETROOT	4	12 x 12 ins (30 x 30 cm)	Plant out at first true leaf. Technique suitable for round-rooted vars only
BRUSSELS SPROUT	2	30 x 30 ins (75 x 75 cm)	
CALABRESE	3–5	12 x 12 ins (30 x 30 cm)	
CARROT	3–5	6 x 6 ins (15 x 15 cm)	Plant out at first true leaf stage. Technique suitable for stump-rooted vars only
CABBAGE	3	24 x 24 ins (60 x 60 cm)	
COURGETTE	2–3	36 x 36 ins (90 x 90 cm)	Propagate in 3 in. (75 mm) pots
DWARF FRENCH BEANS	6	8 x 8 ins (20 x 20 cm)	Propagate in 3 in. (75 mm) pots
HERBS	6	6 x 6 ins (15 x 15 cm)	
KOHL RABI	3–5	8 x 8 ins (20 x 20 cm)	Variety Rowel gives best results
LEEKS	3–5	8 x 8 ins (20 x 20 cm)	
LETTUCE	3	12 x 12 ins (30 x 30 cm)	Technique is best used for loose-leaf and compact varieties e.g. Little Gem
ONIONS	6–8	12 x 12 ins (30 x 30 cm)	Use for normal and over-wintering vars
PEAS	6	8 x 8 ins (20 x 20 cm)	Propagate in 3 in. (75 mm) pots
RUNNER BEANS	3	8 ins (20 cm) apart in rows	Propagate in 3 in. (75 mm) pots
SPINACH	3–5	6 x 6 ins (15 x 15 cm)	
SPRING ONIONS	10–12	4 x 4 ins (10 x 10 cm)	
SWEET CORN	3	30 x 30 ins (75 x 75 cm)	Propagate in 3 in. (75 mm) pots
TURNIP	3–5	12 x 12 ins (30 x 30 cm)	

draw hoe to make a shallow groove (or drill) in the soil, and instead of sowing the seed straight into it, put the peat or vermiculite in first, and sow the seed on top of that. This way, seedlings put down their first roots into something that provides a much better rooting medium than plain soil. This technique is not a substitute for normal soil improvement and cultivation, but by lining the seed drills in this way, you are making a little (expensive) material go a long way, by putting it right where it is needed.

If you have soil that is prone to 'capping' (i.e. which forms a crust on top as it dries out after rain, that tends to be lifted up on the top of emerging seedlings), then you'll find a slight variation on the above idea will give you much better germination of outdoor-sown seeds. That is to put a thin layer of peat or vermiculite *over* the seeds, instead of covering them with soil as usual. This will make it impossible for the soil to 'cap' over the seedlings, and as this prevents a good many of them from coming up, you'll immediately get a much better stand of seedlings.

Fluid Drilling

If you don't mind going to a little more trouble to get *every* possible vegetable from your rows, you can go one step further and use another relatively new technique – fluid drilling, or fluid sowing. The idea here is that seeds are germinated in ideal conditions before you put them into the ground. So, although it can be used for any varieties, it is especially useful for seeds that are slow to germinate in cold soil, or which can have germination problems – like parsley, which germinates best at a temperature of 70°F (21°C), and lettuce, which only germinates below 70°F (21°C). The most practical way of germinating seed for fluid drilling is on damp tissue paper, indoors. Put a layer of tissue paper in the bottom of a waterproof plastic tray or box, sprinkle the seed evenly over it and drip water carefully on until the tissue is saturated, but not awash. Keep the seeds somewhere they receive light (some seeds won't germinate in the dark) but out of direct sunlight. A temperature of about 60–70°F (15–21°C) will suit most seeds. Check them daily to see if the tissue needs re-moistening – if it dries out while the seeds are germinating, it is usually too late to save them. When the seed has just germinated and you can see the first tiny bit of root beginning to emerge – but before it is $\frac{1}{8}$ in. (3 mm) long – (this takes from 24 hours to a few

6

days), mix up some wallpaper glue (the sort without fungicide) into a thick paste and tip the germinated seeds into it. Mix them gently in, and then load the mixture into a cake icing bag with the nozzle removed. Meanwhile have your vegetable plot already prepared, with shallow drills marked out with a draw hoe. On less than perfect soil you could beneficially line the drill with peat or vermiculite as before. Then 'sow' the seeds by squeezing a steady stream of the paste mixture into your seed drills. Cover with soil, peat or vermiculite as usual; otherwise the paste can dry out, taking the seedlings with it.

GROWING TECHNIQUES

Quite apart from plant-raising methods, there are several useful growing techniques you can use to improve productivity from a small plot.

Soil Improvement

This is the most basic, but probably the single most important contributor to raising throughput from a small plot. Unless the soil is already in very good heart, it is beneficial to add bulky organic matter such as well-rotted manure, garden compost, spent hops, mushroom compost, or peat. On soil that is clearly far from ideal, such as very light sandy soils or heavy clay, the regular addition of organic matter is essential, because without it crops will not realise anything like their full potential. The best time to add bulky organic matter is traditionally in the autumn. If, however, the weather is very wet then, and particularly if you garden on heavy soil, it is better to keep off the ground rather than risk compacting it by treading it down when it is soft. You can delay adding organic matter until spring, but in this case it is better not to use manure or garden compost. Peat or 'secondhand' compost from old growing bags is better then because it is already thoroughly decomposed, and can even be used where you want to grow root crops such as carrots, which normally split if they are grown in freshly manured soil.

Deep Beds

Even better than adding organic matter along with the annual digging, the traditional way, is to grow your crops in deep or raised beds. These may be filled with pure compost (which must be very well rotted), or a mixture of soil and compost. Beds of this sort are an incredibly productive way of growing vegetables in a small garden because you can plant at much closer spacings than usual. For a start, you do not need to leave paths between rows of crops. Provided the beds are narrow enough, you can reach to plant, water and weed from the edges, without treading on the soil at all. This means you automatically save about half the space that goes to waste in a normal vegetable garden. But because the beds are not trodden on, and are particularly deeply prepared (by double digging), roots can penetrate downwards instead of having to spread outwards, so you can space plants quite a bit closer together in the rows as well. The ideal spacing allows plants to start touching by the time they are about half grown; roughly two-thirds the spacing normally recommended. So not only do you get a very dense concentration of crops packed into a relatively small space, but also the plants need very little weeding as the shade created by the growing crops is enough to smother out most annual weeds.

There is very little difference between a deep bed and a raised bed: a deep bed is level with the surrounding soil, prepared by digging lots of organic matter into deep trenches in the soil; and a raised bed is made by building up retaining walls of brick or planks above the ground, and filling the space with organic matter, either 'straight' or mixed with soil. On normally good soil, a deep bed works very well, but where the sub-soil is heavy clay this should not be brought to the surface by deep digging, and a raised bed would be better. Raised beds are also better on ground that lies wet in winter, as they enable the soil in them to drain freely. And from a practical point of view, they are also handy if you have difficulty bending.

The actual day-to-day business of growing in either deep or raised beds is a little different from usual, largely because you are growing plants at a much greater density. With so many plants packed in a small space, normal rainfall, which might have been adequate for traditionally spaced crops, won't be enough for such intensively grown crops, and regular watering will be necessary during the summer. Raised beds are particularly prone to drying out fast in warm weather and need checking regularly – especially if you are growing crops like cauliflower, celery or Chinese cabbage that are notoriously quick to bolt if they go short of water. Regular feeding will also be necessary to obtain the best results. In addition to using a base fertiliser dressing before sowing or planting, it is a good idea to 'top up' by liquid feeding and foliar feeding once every week or two from the time crops are half grown to keep them growing steadily all of the time.

Crop Protection

Some sort of protection from wind and cold is specially useful for growing early and late crops, though it can be a great help during the summer as well if you are aiming for peak productivity. The traditional way of protecting crops is by covering them with cloches. Cloches not only produce earlier and faster growing crops, but they also mean a greater proportion of what you grow is usable. By protecting plants from cold wind and rain, as well as cats, dogs, birds and a lot of other pests, the end result is generally of higher quality – clean, unmarked vegetables with little going to waste when they are prepared for cooking.

Cloches are traditionally used to extend the growing season, allowing you to grow crops much earlier and later in the year than would be possible without cover. And although they are normally used to get newly sown or planted crops off to a good start, cloches can be left over low-growing subjects like lettuce, right up until they are picked. But glass, and even plastic, cloches can be expensive to buy, notoriously easy to break, and take up valuable storage space when they are not in use. A much better way of doing the same job in a small garden, is to use floating cloches instead. A floating cloche is nothing more than a sheet of perforated polythene film, which is laid on the soil where seeds have been sown, or seedlings planted. As the plants grow, the cloche lifts up, supported by the plants underneath it. The plastic allows the temperature to build up beneath it like in a normal cloche, and in the same way it protects plants from wind, cold and animals etc. Like an ordinary cloche, it can be used for a few weeks to get crops off to a good start, or it can be left in place over low crops until they are cut. What is special about floating cloches is that they are much cheaper to buy than the usual sort; the plastic sheet comes in a length that you can cut to fit whatever size of bed you want, and is cheap enough to throw away after using it once (although it can, in fact, be re-used several times). It is supplied in lengths sufficient to re-cover a small vegetable plot several times over, so a pack goes quite a long way.

Laying a floating cloche is very little more trouble than moving

9

a row of normal cloches. If you grow in a raised bed with plank sides, the floating cloche can simply be laid over it and pinned in place with drawing pins. In a level bed, the polythene can be held in position with a row of bricks or planks laid round the edges, or you can take out a shallow trench with a draw hoe and bury the edge of the plastic in it.

Since the polythene is perforated, there is no need to remove the floating cloche for watering – just use the hose as if the cloche was not there. (You will probably need to lift a corner of the cloche to see if watering is needed.) It should not be necessary to weed underneath the cloche provided you sow or plant into weed-free soil in the first place, and only intend to leave it in place until the crop is partly grown. If you plan leaving it down for most – or all – of the time until the vegetables are harvested, you may need to do a little weeding. In this case, the cloche must be rolled back off the crop and replaced after you have finished working. You will probably not need to weed more than once or twice though; if you space plants fairly close together (as for instance on a deep bed) you will find plants soon touching each other, at which point they will be able to smother out any weeds that try to grow.

Now that floating cloches have become widely accepted, a new version has been brought out. The idea is very similar, but instead of using a sheet of perforated polythene to cover the crops, a very light fabric made of fine woven polythene fibres is used instead. This is popularly known as 'fleece', and is sold under several different trade names. It works in exactly the same way as a floating cloche, and like it, allows water and air to pass through its tiny perforations. But – so it is claimed – it also gives several degrees of frost protection to plants growing under it, so you should be able to plant slightly earlier than usual. Like plastic, fleece can be re-used several times.

Both fleece and floating cloches can be used on a much smaller scale, cut to the appropriate size, to wrap over crops growing in pots or growing bags – a useful extra in a small space. Fleece can also be laid over greenhouse plants on cold nights in winter, or even to make a sort of thermal curtain for greenhouse lining.

Inter-cropping and Catch-cropping

These are both very useful techniques for making the most of a limited space. Inter-cropping means growing a fast crop between two rows of a slower one, for instance radish sown between two rows of Brussels sprout plants – the radish being sown at the same time as the plants are put in, but harvested long before the brassicas fill the rows. Catch-cropping means growing a fast crop like lettuce in the soil while it is otherwise vacant, perhaps at the start or finish of the season, or in the interval between pulling out winter brassicas and being able to plant frost-tender plants such as marrows or sweet corn. By using a combination of the two techniques, it should be possible to keep the vegetable patch full of growing crops all the time. And although neither inter-cropping nor catch-cropping are new techniques, they are ones that have tended to fall into disuse over the years – though now that so many people with small gardens are taking to vegetable growing, interest in them is fast gaining ground. New work has been done at organisations like the National Vegetable Research Station (now part of the Institute of Horticultural Research), which offers a few interesting suggestions for suitable crops to inter-plant, so you can design yourself a garden cropping plan that fits together like pieces of a jigsaw.

Suitable crops for catch-cropping are generally fast-growing – lettuce, radish, kohl rabi, spinach, baby turnips and early carrots for instance. But by planting pot-grown plants instead of sowing seed directly into the ground, you can shorten the time other crops need to occupy the ground, enabling you to grow things like French beans, peas, baby beet, calabrese, or leafy herbs as catch-crops too. Catch-crops are generally quite easy to plan for – you can see where a gap will appear when, for instance, a row of cauliflowers are beginning to head up, and have your lettuce plants all ready to go in when the caulis come out. Lettuce plants in summer take 6–8 weeks to mature, so a couple of weeks after planting them, you can be sowing the next crop to go into the space.

Inter-cropping is a bit more complicated to plan for, because you are doing what amounts to growing three rows of crops in the space meant for two. As stated, this is done by growing a fast one between two rows of slow ones. Traditionally the fastest crops, such as lettuce, radish, baby turnips and spinach, were always inter-planted – this was and still is very useful in small spaces, since it means you don't have to allocate any particular part of the vegetable plot to them, you just fit them in wherever there's room between other things. They sit very comfortably, for instance, between rows of summer cabbage planted in spring, runner beans planted in May or June, outdoor tomatoes planted in June, and

11

Brussels sprouts, savoys, kale, winter cabbage and cauliflowers planted in June and July. But now the experts have come up with more interesting combinations. Two that they find particularly successful are French beans sown between sweet corn, and early carrots sown between parsnips. The important thing is to choose crops that have the same growing requirements, and where, although you sow or plant both crops at the same time, one will be ready long before the other.

SPECIALLY FAST VARIETIES FOR CATCH- AND INTER-CROPPING

BEETROOT – 'Replata', a naturally very early, fast variety, can be had even faster by sowing in February in small pots in the propagator (sow multi-seeded if you like).

CALABRESE – most varieties are fairly fast growing, but 'Dandy Early' is very quick to mature and can be sown in spring or summer; plant out from pots for fastest results.

CARROT – all early varieties mature fast, especially 'Nantes Express', 'Nantes Frubund', 'Rondo' and 'Amsterdam Forcing'.

CORN SALAD – all varieties; use thinnings from the time they have two true leaves; remainder grows into small rosettes in a few weeks.

DWARF FRENCH BEAN – especially 'Aramis' (pencil bean).

HERBS – leafy annuals such as Chervil, Basil, Sweet Marjoram, Summer Savory, Coriander and Dill.

KOHL RABI – variety 'Rowel' is best flavoured; unlike other kohl rabi it must be transplanted to do well.

LETTUCE – especially miniature varieties, e.g. 'Little Gem', 'Tom Thumb'.

RADISH – all mature quickly, but 'Saxa Short Top', 'Ribella' are specially fast.

SPINACH – all varieties mature fast.

TURNIP – 'Tokyo Cross', 'Snowball', 'Milan White Forcing'.

PLANNING AND ORGANISING THE VEGETABLE PLOT

When space is limited, one way of making the most of it is by planning what you are going to grow where and when in reasonable detail before starting to plant. That way, you can be sure you have room for all the different things you want to grow, besides having a good idea when you will need to start propagating each batch of plants. It also helps you to see where and when catch-crops or inter-crops fit into your scheme.

It is best to create your own plan based on what vegetables you and your family like most, and in what sort of quantities – in a small space this makes much more sense than just following a traditional allotment-style cropping plan, which is aimed at providing enough of everything to feed a family for a whole year.

But besides planning what you want to grow there are a few practical considerations to take into account – such as crop rotation, and how to cope if there just is not enough room in the vegetable garden – or worse still, no proper vegetable garden at all.

Crop Rotation

In planning the cropping of any vegetable garden, one thing that needs to be taken into account is crop rotation. Basically, the idea of crop rotation is to group together vegetables with similar cultural requirements – those that require lime or manure, and those that dislike lime or manure. You can rotate the different groups of crops round your plot so you don't grow the same kind of vegetables in the same bit of ground two years running. There are several good reasons for doing this. One is to avoid getting a build-up of the sort of soil-borne pests and diseases that affect a particular crop, since the crop is moved every year. Another is that you slowly but surely work your way right round the plot improving the soil without having to tackle the whole lot in one year. And last, but most important, you can still grow the full range of crops as you are taking care of all their different cultivation requirements.

Traditionally, vegetable plots were divided into three or even four sections for purposes of crop rotation. One section would be allocated to root vegetables, another to brassicas, and a third to peas, beans, salads and everything else. Sometimes the plot would even be split into four, with the fourth part put down entirely to potatoes, as they take such a lot of room. Each of these sections would be prepared according to what was going to be planted in it. The plot for brassicas would receive fertiliser and lime; those for potatoes and root vegetables would be given

A **'GREENS'**	**B** **'GREENS'**

A   'GREENS'

LATE MAY/EARLY JUNE
plant: Brussels sprout
      Summer cabbages
      Cauliflowers
      Runner beans

JULY
plant: Savoys
      Autumn cauliflowers
      Broccoli
      Winter cabbages

AUGUST/SEPTEMBER
plant: Spring cabbages

CATCH-CROPS
      Early peas
      Broad beans

INTER-CROPS
      Lettuce
      Spinach

B   'GREENS'

APRIL
sow: Broad beans
     Sugar peas

JUNE
plant: Calabrese
     Broccoli 'romanesco'
     Red cabbage
     White cabbage Minicole
sow: New Zealand
      spinach
     Purslane

JULY
sow: Chinese cabbage
     Pak choi
     Swiss chard
     Radicchio

AUGUST/SEPTEMBER
sow: Corn salad

SEPTEMBER
plant: Over-wintering onions

INTER-CROP/CATCH-CROP
Lettuce Little Gem, Tom Thumb
Florence fennel
Dwarf French beans

ROOTS

MARCH
plant: Onion sets

APRIL
plant: Early potatoes
sow: Early beetroot
     Early carrot
     Parsnips

MAY
plant: Leeks
sow: Maincrop beetroot
     Maincrop carrot

JUNE
sow: Swedes

INTER-CROP
     Lettuce
     Spinach
     Radish
     Spring onion
     Early carrot

ROOTS

MARCH
plant: Shallots
     Garlic
     Jerusalem artichokes

APRIL
plant: Early potatoes
sow: Hamburg parsley
     Salsify
     Scorzonera

INTER-CROP/CATCH-CROP
     Kohl rabi
     Baby beetroot
     Radish
     Spring onion
     Finger carrots
     Baby turnips

**GROWING BAGS
ON PATIO**

Tomatoes
Outdoor cucumbers

**GROWING BAGS
ON PATIO**

Cherry tomatoes
Outdoor cucumbers
Golden courgettes
Mixed herbs

SMALL VEGETABLE PLANNER

Plan for a very intensive small vegetable plot – a raised or deep bed roughly divided into two, half for brassicas and things it is appropriate or convenient to grow with them, and the other for root crops.

The bed is well prepared to start with by digging lots of well rotted organic matter in during the autumn. If manure is used this should only be used on the half where brassicas will grow; treat the root end with peat or very thoroughly rotted garden compost. Each year alternate the ends, and 'top' up the organic content of the brassica end by digging in more well rotted material. Avoid replanting the same crops in exactly the same positions each time you 'change ends' – alter the position of individual rows of plants as much as you can to avoid growing the same crops in the same bit of ground.

PLAN A is for a traditional selection of crops.

PLAN B shows a gourmet choice, using vegetables that taste best fresh-grown, or which cost most to buy – it ignores those that are cheap and plentiful in the shops.

---

fertiliser only, and that for peas, beans, salads and odds and ends like tomatoes and spinach would get manure only. This is, to say the least, not terribly practical in a small garden.

A much more workable alternative is to prepare all the ground as well as possible when you first start your vegetable garden, and from then on try to keep brassicas and root crops at separate ends of the plot which are swapped over every year, with salads, spinach and other oddments fitted in between as catch- or inter-crops. Tomatoes, and anything else that does not fit in, can always be grown in pots on the patio. The most important thing is to get the soil well prepared in the first place, particularly if it has not been regularly cultivated before. To do this, it is worth using a lot of organic matter on the whole plot to get the maximum improvement in the shortest possible time. Use a barrowful of manure or compost per square yard (metre), or more if you can. This should be dug in during the autumn. Manuring the whole plot at once does prevent you from growing root crops the first year, as they tend to fork if they are grown in freshly manured soil. But if you particularly want to grow them, you could always prepare the soil where they are to be sown with peat or old growing-bag compost instead. Don't use lime on the plot unless it is really essential – small soil tests, which are inexpensive and readily available in garden centres, tell you at once if you need to lime your soil. Lime was frequently used just because it was traditional, regardless of whether it was actually needed or not – and more often than not, it isn't. Another common reason for using lime was because soil was infected by club-root. As a remedy, it does not work very well, and nor does any other – at best, club-root remedies only slow down the attack of the club-root organism. If you garden on ground with club-root, it is much better to either give up growing brassicas and grow more of other things, or, where practical, to grow your brassicas in large containers or growing bags.

Growing Vegetables without a Vegetable Garden

If you don't have much room for a conventional vegetable garden, then growing bags, large pots or patio containers are a convenient and practical alternative. Containers make crops portable, so you can start them under glass if you want, and move them out to the patio later, or shift them about the garden as necessary. They also make it possible to turn any vacant hard surface into a productive vegetable patch – concrete, paving or gravel. You can even grow vegetables on balconies or on flat roofs if normal garden space is short, by using containers. The only limiting factors are sun (vegetables need to be in sun at least half the day), shelter (few crops do well in exposed locations), weight (containers of moist compost are not light, so if you put them on a roof make sure it is built to take the weight), and whether you can get at the containers easily to look after them. This is specially important, because grown in such limited root run, crops tend to dry out much more quickly than those grown in the garden, and consequently you can expect to do very much more watering than usual. You will also need to feed very regularly too.

If you are growing vegetables in pots or patio containers, the best idea is to treat them rather like pot plants. Plant them in a pot that is an appropriate size for the eventual size of plant; you can grow single plants in large pots, or several plants of one kind in a bigger container – it is not a good idea to mix different crops in the same tub. Use good potting compost or a multi-purpose compost, not garden soil, to fill the container – proper potting compost provides a much better root environment for this very intensive form of growing. Check the compost every day by sticking your finger in it to see if it needs watering, and aim to keep the compost just moist all of the time. To feed, add a dose of general-purpose liquid or soluble feed to the water once or twice a week, starting about four weeks after planting and continuing until a week or two before you pick the crop.

(ABOVE) Container scheme for a sunny corner using a mixture of flowering and foliage plants.

(RIGHT) Small courtyard style garden, all paving and gravel on the ground, plus a tiny fountain playing up through an old mill stone to provide movement, sparkle and sounds.

Successful plant combination for a shady spot – rhododendron, hardy
fern and ladies mantle (Alchemilla mollis).

(RIGHT) Unusual compact water feature; a glass 'fountain', where water leaks out from between layers of strata, and runs away into the surrounding gravel. As there is no depth of water, this idea is perfectly safe in a garden where small children may be left playing without supervision.

(BELOW) Cottage-style garden. Note the crowded, natural look, with no conventional lawns, only paths running through between plants. An old wheelbarrow has been turned into an attractive rustic container for plants.

Collection of herbs that are both ornamental and edible growing in
multi-storey container.

If using growing bags, the instructions provided with them normally cover the more usual crops, such as tomatoes, but rarely mention others – though lots of vegetables can be grown very successfully in bags. The technique is not difficult. Basically a growing bag is just a larger container. Plant the bags at the same time as you would normally set vegetables out in the garden, or a couple of weeks earlier if you are starting the crop under glass. Normally, pot-grown plants should be planted in growing bags, but some crops with large seeds, such as peas, beans and spinach, can be sown directly into the bags. Cut out the whole front of the bag, and either sow a series of parallel rows across the compost, or scatter the seed evenly over the surface. Even root crops can be grown in bags, provided you choose those that don't have long tap roots as they would deform when they touched the bottom of the bag. When they come up, thin the seedlings out to a suitable spacing.

PLANTS PER GROWING BAG:

AUBERGINES – 3–4.

BEANS, BROAD – 16.

BEANS, FRENCH – 24.

BEANS, RUNNER – 16.

BEETROOT (round-rooted varieties only, such as 'Boltardy', 'Replata') – sow broadcast and thin to 3–4 ins (7.5–10 cm) apart, or plant seedlings in peat pots.

CABBAGE 6–8 of a compact variety such as 'Hispi' or 'Pixie'.

CALABRESE – 10–12.

CARROT (stump-rooted varieties such as 'Rondo') – sow broadcast and thin to 3 ins (7.5 cm) apart.

CHARD, SWISS OR RHUBARB – 10.

COURGETTE – 3.

CORN SALAD – sow broadcast and thin to 3 ins (7.5 cm) apart.

CUCUMBERS – 4–6.

KOHL RABI – sow broadcast and thin to 6 ins (15 cm) apart.

LETTUCE – 8, or up to 12 of a compact variety like 'Little Gem'.

MELONS – 4–6.

ONIONS – 20–plant sets or seedlings.

PEAS – 24–30.

PEPPERS – 6.

POTATOES – 8–10 (only early varieties are worth growing).

SPINACH – sow broadcast and thin to 3 ins (7.5 cm) apart.

SPRING ONIONS – sow broadcast and thin to 1–2 ins (2.5–5 cm) apart.

SWEET CORN – 8.

TOMATOES – 3–4.

TURNIP (summer varieties) – sow broadcast, thin to 2–3 ins (5–7.5 cm) apart.

WATERCRESS – plant rooted cuttings taken from a greengrocer's bunch 6 ins (15 cm) apart, or sow seed direct into the bag and thin. Keep very moist. Very successful in growing bags.

Growing Vegetables in Flower Beds

Yet another way of fitting vegetables into a garden that doesn't otherwise have room to grow them, is by infiltrating the flower beds. To do this successfully, it is essential to choose the more ornamental varieties – and some are surprisingly so. You can have climbing crops like runner beans, peas and purple climbing beans growing on a fence, wall, or over cane 'wigwams' in a border; herbs can sit quite happily amongst cottage-garden plants; or try red-leaved beetroot, ornamental cabbage, red frilly lettuce and red rhubarb chard for their foliage effect amongst bedding plants, as well as the larger and showier globe artichokes (like giant thistle heads), Jerusalem artichokes (similar to sunflowers) with herbaceous plants and shrubs.

For growing mixed edible and ornamental beds, prepare the soil as you would for annual flowers, but avoid using manure where you plan to grow root vegetables – use peat there instead, and mark the spots with canes so you know where they are. Then either sow or plant.

A lot of seeds of the more ornamental vegetables are not commonly available in garden centres, and if you plan this approach it is well worthwhile sending off for your (free) copies of the large seed firms' catalogues which you can then order from.

Suitable varieties include:

ARTICHOKE, GLOBE – most have green heads but there is also a violet variety, 'Violetta di Chioggia'. Edible flower buds, picked while still tightly closed over a long season, late spring and summer.

ARTICHOKE, JERUSALEM – variety 'Dwarf Sunray' is 2 ft (60 cm) shorter than most, at around 5 ft (120 cm). Plants look like sunflowers; edible tuberous roots are harvested late autumn.

ASPARAGUS PEA – unusual vegetable with pea-like foliage and bright red pea flowers, followed by winged pods which are lightly cooked and used whole. Not a heavy cropper but an interesting gourmet vegetable.

BEETROOT – the old variety 'Bull's Blood' has bright red leaves. Use for pickling, or pull young to use fresh.

BRUSSELS SPROUT – 'Rubine', the sprout equivalent of red cabbage, has purpley-red leaves and similarly coloured sprouts, which are small and delicious. Another gourmet vegetable, but a light cropper.

CABBAGE – red cabbages look pretty enough to grow in the flower bed; the ornamental cabbage with colourful pink, green and white variegated leaves is also edible.

CHARD – second cousin of Swiss chard is a spectacular bright red stemmed version called 'Rhubarb Chard', and the less hardy 'Rainbow Chard' which comes in a mixture of yellow, red and white stems. Both stems and leaves are edible, though usually cooked separately, the leaves being used much like spinach.

CLIMBING FRENCH BEANS – 'Purple Podded' and other similar varieties look most ornamental. Grow on sheds, fences, trellis or a wigwam of canes.

CUCUMBER – the outdoor variety 'Crystal Apple' produces lots of small, round, well-flavoured bright yellow fruit; plants look nicest trained over a wigwam of canes. Useful for adding height to a border, and carries a good crop. Use like normal cucumber.

DWARF FRENCH BEANS – purple podded are the most ornamental; varieties available include 'Royal Burgundy', 'Purple Queen' and 'Blue Coco'. Pods turn green when cooked.

HERBS – most varieties can be grown inconspicuously in the flower garden; those that are most useful as well as most ornamental are Basil 'Dark Opal' or 'Fluffy Ruffles' (purple-red leaves), Rosemary, Chives, Dill, Fennel, French Sorrel, Summer Savory, Thyme, Marjoram and Curly-leaved Parsley.

ICE PLANT (*Mesembryanthemum crystallinum*) – a close relative of the bedding Mesembryanthemum, this is grown for its leaves which are delicious in salads, crispy with a hint of salt. Makes an attractive and unusual foliage plant for a sunny spot; the leaves are covered in sparkly raised bumps looking like dew. Grow in patches and pick a few shoots leaving the rest of the plant to grow.

KOHL RABI – 'Purple Vienna' may be the most ornamental, but any kohl rabi looks interesting in the flower border – it produces a tennis-ball-like 'root' in light green or mauve with short, rather waxy-looking leaves to match. Use like a turnip (though much better tasting) while still young and tender.

LAMB'S LETTUCE – sow in autumn; produces small, low, rosette-shaped plants that provide good ground cover; pick through the winter to use as salad.

LETTUCE – loose-leaf (often called 'cut and come again') varieties, such as 'Salad Bowl', 'Red Salad Bowl' and 'Lollo', last all summer as they don't form a heart – you just pick off the leaves you want; look like shaggy mop-heads in red or green – most ornamental and unusual.

NASTURTIUM – grow any variety of ordinary hardy annual bedding Nasturtium, and use the leaves and flowers in salads.

ORACHE – unusual vegetable used like spinach, available in red or yellow versions both of which are extremely pretty. Grows tall and upright, makes a good foliage plant between bedding. Pick individual leaves to cook, or snap the heads off young plants leaving the rest to re-sprout.

PEAS – Mangetout and snap peas (that are cooked pod and all) look quite attractive growing up twigs; 'Purple Podded' lives up to its name, and is prettier still. More unusual is 'Bikini', which produces very few leaves, but masses of tightly curled tendrils instead – plus normal peas.

RUNNER BEANS – all have pretty flowers, usually red; 'Painted Lady' has red and white flowers.

SQUASHES – marrow-like plants which produce fruit just like gourds, but edible. Leave on the plants till autumn to ripen, then store and use in winter. Some kinds can also be used fresh in summer while young. Varieties available include 'Vegetable spaghetti', 'Table Ace', 'Custard White' (shaped like custard pies), 'Sunburst' (bright yellow custard-pie-shaped fruit). Allow to trail over walls or train up trellis.

SPECIALLY PRODUCTIVE VARIETIES

It's not only how you grow, it's what you grow that makes all the difference in a small garden. Plant breeders are increasingly coming up with new varieties designed to be planted closer together than usual, which crop heavier, mature faster, produce better crops in a cold summer, or which are suitable for freezing – all aimed at making it possible to get more than ever from a small plot. You can do even better by growing dual-purpose crops, which give you two different vegetables from one plant. So here are some suggestions for varieties to grow for peak productivity.

Compact Varieties

Modern horticultural research has shown that any varieties, grown slightly closer together than usual, will give you a heavier weight of crops from a given area. The individual vegetables will be smaller than usual, but because there are more of them, you'll more than make up the difference. But if you want really intensive production, choose compact varieties – on well-prepared soil, and especially on deep beds, you should be able to plant them at a third to one half of the spacing normally recommended for standard varieties.

BEETROOT – 'Detroit Little Ball'.
BROAD BEAN – 'The Sutton', 'Bonny Lad'.
BRUSSELS SPROUT – 'Asmer Monitor'.
CABBAGE – 'Hispi', 'Quickstep', 'April', 'Pixie', 'Minicole', 'Christmas Drumhead'.
CALABRESE – 'Dandy Early'.
CARROT – 'Suko' (finger carrot).
CAULIFLOWER – 'Snowball'; mini varieties – 'Garant', 'Predominant' (space 6 x 6 ins/15 x 15 cm).
COURGETTE – 'Gold Rush'.
CUCUMBER (outdoor) – 'Bush Crop'.
LETTUCE, hearting – 'Little Gem', 'Tom Thumb'.
LETTUCE, loose leafe – 'Salad Bowl', 'Lollo'.
RED CABBAGE – 'Langedijker Early'.
SAVOY – 'Spivoy'.
SWEET CORN – 'Butter Imp', dwarf plants 2 ft 6 ins (75 cm) tall producing half-size cobs, for close spacing.

Heavy-cropping Varieties

Some varieties of any vegetable are naturally more productive than others, but there are also some kinds of vegetable that are particularly worthwhile growing where space is short as they produce so much more usable food from the space than others.

21

ASPARAGUS – the new all-male varieties, such as 'Lucullus', are much more productive than old varieties that contain a mix of male and female plants – the females produce berries in autumn, and not such good spears in spring.

BEETROOT – old-fashioned 'tankard' beetroot produce much more beetroot per row than round- or taper-rooted varieties; tankard beet have large, upright, cylindrical roots which form above ground; few varieties still exist, the most widely available is 'Cylindra'.

BROAD BEAN – 'Witkein Major', a heavy cropper and an early producer.

BRUSSELS SPROUT – new F1 hybrid varieties should produce twice the weight of crop of traditional varieties; particularly good are 'Achilles', 'Peer Gynt', 'Sentinel', 'Citadel'.

COURGETTE – 'Ambassador'. Green varieties produce heavier crops than golden courgettes. Pick regularly for maximum productivity.

CUCUMBERS – all are very productive and crop from about 4–6 weeks after planting till the start of cold weather in autumn; small-fruited kinds, like 'Fembaby' and 'Patio Pik', have cucumbers ready to cut more often than full-sized kinds which take longer to develop. Each plant can produce thirty or more cucumbers in a season.

LEEKS – useful as they let you pack a lot of vegetable into each row, especially giant varieties such as 'Molos', 'Wila' and 'Catalina'.

PEAS – snap and mangetout varieties go much further than normal peas as you cook and eat them complete with pods.

RUNNER BEANS – runners produce much heavier crops and over a far longer period than French beans; any climbing beans produce more than dwarf varieties as they have more stem from which to do so. 'Goliath' is a particularly productive runner bean. Pick runner beans daily for maximum crops.

Fast-maturing Varieties

Crops that mature quickly and are suitable for catch- or inter-cropping have been covered elsewhere. But with vegetables that normally remain in the ground for some time before they produce a crop, such as sweet corn, it is often useful to grow the faster-maturing varieties. The quicker 'turn round' this gives can often save enough time to fit an extra crop into your cropping plan. But in some cases – for instance when growing sweet corn in the north of the country – it is only by growing a fast-maturing variety that the crop will mature reliably before the end of the season.

BEETROOT – 'Replata', 'Boltardy'.

BROAD BEAN – 'Witkiem Major'.

CABBAGE – 'Quickstep', 'Hispi'.

CALABRESE – 'Mercedes', 'Green Comet', 'Emperor'.

CARROT – all early varieties mature fast, especially 'Nantes Express', 'Nantes Frubund', 'Rondo', 'Amsterdam Forcing', and can also be sown in late summer for a fast autumn crop of new carrots.

CAULIFLOWER – 'Snow King', 'Snow Crown' (sow April, cut $2\frac{1}{2}$ months later).

CHINESE GREENS – Chinese cabbage, Pak Choi.

DWARF FRENCH BEAN – 'Aramis'.

MELON – 'Sweetheart', small cantaloupe melons very fast to ripen.

SAVOY – 'Spivoy'.

SWEET CORN – 'Polar Vee', 'Early Extra Sweet', 'Sundance'.

Freezer Varieties

The freezer is, of course, invaluable for enabling you to store gluts of garden produce you would not normally have been able to eat fresh. But it can also contribute enormously to the productivity of your garden. By growing freezer varieties (usually marked with an asterisk in the seed catalogues), you can often clear an entire crop virtually all at once and free the ground to grow something else, instead of picking a little at a time over a long period to use fresh. This is particularly useful with summer crops. But there is also an advantage in growing freezer varieties of winter vegetables if you choose those that mature early, so your crop can be picked and safely in the freezer before the start of bad weather which could mark or spoil it. It also makes life easier for you, as there is no tramping down the garden to pick winter vegetables in cold, windy or rainy weather.

The following are freezer varieties that are particularly useful to help you achieve greater productivity from the garden:

BEETROOT – 'Boltardy', 'Cylindra'.

BROAD BEAN – 'Witkiem Major' (very early variety, ready to pick at the same time as autumn-sown beans).

BRUSSELS SPROUT – 'Sentinel' (ready August–September).

CALABRESE – 'Green Comet', 'Emperor', 'Dandy Early'.

CARROT – 'Rondo', 'Suko', 'Nantes Express'.

CAULIFLOWER – 'Snow King', 'Alpha', 'Snowball'; mini-caulis – 'Garant' and 'Predominant'.

COURGETTES – 'Gold Rush'.

FRENCH BEANS – 'Aramis' and most other varieties.

LEEK – 'King Richard', long thin stems (ready September–November).

SNAP PEAS – 'Sugar Snap', 'Oregon Sugar Pod'.

SPINACH – most varieties but not New Zealand Spinach or spinach beet.

PEA – semi-leafless peas 'Bikini', 'Poppet' and most normal varieties.

SWEET CORN – 'Polar Vee', 'Early Extra Sweet', 'Butter Imp', 'Sundance'.

Multi-purpose Crops

These are specially handy where space is really short as they give you two different crops in the space of one.

BRUSSELS SPROUT – any variety of sprout produces 'sprout tops' (rather like spring cabbage) at the top of the stem in early spring as well as having sprouts along the stem itself; variety 'Ormavon' is particularly prolific with its tops, producing what is virtually cabbage at the top, as well as a good crop of sprouts.

CELTUCE – lettuce-like plants with thick mid-ribs; leaves used as lettuce and stems as celery. Easy to grow and well flavoured. Can also be used in Chinese cookery.

FLORENCE FENNEL – use leaves as fennel herb, swollen stems like celery (faintly aniseed flavoured) braised or raw in salads.

PEAS – semi-leafless varieties, such as 'Bikini' and 'Poppet', can be used not only for peas, but also their tendrils can be steamed as a vegetable or used in Chinese cookery.

SPRING ONION – 'Santa Claus' has pretty red stems, can be used as spring onion or left to grow bigger, when it can be used like a leek.

LEFT Red lettuce growing in growing bags (to make productive use of a wide path) under 'fleece' (to protect them from hail and strong winds early in the season – it also brings them on faster).

BELOW Vegetable seedlings raised 'multi-seeded' in peat pots.

LEFT Intercropping – in this case two rows of winter cropping chicories are separated by two rows of fast-maturing summer salads. Note that although spaced close together, it is still possible to run an onion hoe between the rows.

BELOW Runner beans growing on 'wigwams' (tripods of canes) to save space.

(OPPOSITE PAGE)

TOP Multi-seeded beetroot showing how they jostle for space and avoid becoming square shaped.

BOTTOM Fluid drilling pre-germinated seed using a polythene bag with the corner cut off to squeeze the seed/gel mixture from.

ABOVE Fan-trained gooseberry plant on a wall; alpine strawberries used as ground cover.

(OPPOSITE PAGE)
TOP Espalier-trained pear tree growing against a fence, with alpine strawberries grown as ground cover at its base.
BOTTOM Corner of productive small fruit garden showing cordon-trained apples and fan-trained morello cherry on the fences, alpine strawberries for ground cover.

ABOVE Multi-storey planting – here a climber (golden ivy) has been grown up a conifer that has gone brown at the bottom, hiding the damage.

(OPPOSITE PAGE)
TOP Upright cordon apples; 'pillars' are very space saving.
BOTTOM Standard-trained grape vines are an unusual way of saving space in a small garden.

Very unusual 'oriental' inspired courtyard style garden based on bamboos and gravel. Centrepiece is a bamboo growing in an oriental frost-proof pot.

SWISS CHARD — use green part of leaf as spinach, cook mid-ribs and stems separately and serve with melted butter, rather as you would asparagus (though it doesn't taste anything like asparagus).

Vegetables that Crop Continuously over a Long Period

Long-term crops, from which a single sowing or planting keep you picking regularly over a long season without needing to keep replanting, can also be great time savers.

BRUSSELS SPROUTS — 'Groniger Stiekma' (pick from September to February/March).

COURGETTES — any variety picked regularly will continue to produce regularly throughout the summer. 'Ambassador' is particularly productive.

CUCUMBERS — all cucumbers crop continuously all summer. Small-fruited kinds, such as 'Pepita', produce 'little and often' whereas very large-fruited kinds can have gaps in production between flushes.

HERBS — most can be picked little and often.

LEEKS — 'Molos' (cut from October to January), 'Wila' or 'Blue Solaise' Christmas to April/May.

LETTUCE — loose-leaf or 'cut and come again' varieties such as 'Salad Bowl' (both available in red- or green-leaved forms). Do not produce hearts, but allow you to pick a few leaves and let the rest keep growing.

RUNNER BEANS — pick continuously over most of the summer, far longer cropping season and heavier crops than French beans. Climbing varieties crop much heavier than dwarf kinds.

SPINACH — grow spinach beet which produces new leaves for several months, or New Zealand Spinach, which is not a normal spinach at all but a different plant entirely; has lots of small diamond-shaped leaves, does not bolt even in hot weather and can be picked continuously all summer. Not frost hardy so do not sow or plant it until after May.

Cold-tolerant Varieties

A few of our regular garden crops such as cucumbers, peppers and tomatoes are southern European plants which, with us, are growing at the extreme northern extent of their climatic range. This means that in most summers the crops they produce can be rather disappointing, especially when they are grown out of doors. A lot of modern research is currently going into looking for cold-tolerant varieties that will produce good crops either out of doors or under unheated glass. These are some of the ones to look out for.

CUCUMBER (outdoor) – modern varieties are more like normal cucumbers, not heavily spined like old ridge kinds – 'Bush Crop' (compact bush variety), 'Tokyo Slicer' (train up a wigwam of canes to save space).

CUCUMBER (for cold greenhouse) – 'Athene', 'Diana', 'Mildana', 'Sandra', 'Kyoto'.

MELON – 'Sweetheart'; not a new variety but the one that still grows and ripens best even in a poor summer.

TOMATO (for greenhouse or outdoors) – 'Pixie', 'Tornado', 'Sweet 100', 'Gardeners' Delight', (outdoors) 'Red Alert', 'Outdoor Girl'. NB: cold-tolerant and the very tiny cherry varieties ripen earlier than other varieties giving not only an earlier crop but also a longer cropping season, even in a poor summer. Large beefsteak tomatoes take longest to ripen.

SWEET PEPPERS – 'Canape', 'Gypsy'.

Vegetables to fill the Winter/Spring Gap

Crops that you can plant or sow in late summer after early crops have been cleared, which grow during the late autumn/winter and are ready to use in winter/spring when there is little else about, are particularly valuable in any garden. But in small gardens, they are yet another way of extending your cropping plan all season round, to make the very best use of the space available. Such crops will normally be cleared in good time to sow and plant your usual summer crops.

But there is one very valuable crop that is worth special mention when it comes to making the best use of space when ground is not occupied by other crops, and that is over-wintering onions. These are a relatively new crop that has only been available for a few years. Originally they had to be grown from seed sown in August, but now you can grow them from sets which can be planted any time in the autumn. As their name suggests, over-wintering onions occupy the ground during the winter, when there isn't much else you could be using it for. They are ready to pull in mid-summer, around the end of June and early July, long before 'ordinary' onions can be harvested. By clearing the crop so early, the ground is left free ready to be planted with winter cabbage, cauliflowers, savoys, or kale – besides providing you with a useful crop of onions at a time 'normal' onions are in short supply in the shops.

Over-wintering onions don't keep, so you have to use them within a month of them being ready. However, you don't have to wait for them to ripen like 'keeping' onions – you can start pulling as soon as you find one big enough, from around early May. And they do fill a gap – in both garden and larder – very usefully.

CABBAGE (spring) – sow normal spring cabbage varieties such as 'April', 'Pixie', July/August where they are to crop or transplant; sow 'Hispi' under glass August/September to plant under cloches or cold frame October for cutting April/May, or March for cutting May/June.

CABBAGE (winter) – grow the most frost-resistant varieties, and those that heart up in autumn and 'hold' for several months when ready – Tundra, winter white (coleslaw) cabbage such as 'Holland Late Winter'.

CAULIFLOWER – 'Alpha', sow under glass in September and plant under cloches late autumn or early spring to cut in June.

CHICORY – Belgium chicory ('Whitloof', 'Normato') needs a long growing season and the roots have to be dug and stored, then forced to produce blanched heads of chicory. Other types of chicory are available for use as winter salads; these produce heads like cos lettuce – varieties 'Sugar Loaf', 'Crystal Head', etc. – sow June/July. Another kind of chicory is 'Radichio', which looks like a bright-red iceberg lettuce – varieties 'Red Verona', 'Palla Rossa' – sow June/July, leaves do not turn red till weather gets cold. Soak chicory leaves in tepid water for 2 hours to remove bitter taste when preparing them to eat.

CORN SALAD – sow late summer and autumn, rosettes are very hardy and can be picked throughout winter and early spring as required.

ENDIVE – sow June/July; when hearts form, cover with large flower pot to blanch for a few days, then use like lettuce. Frilly-leaved varieties are most attractive, such as 'Green Curled' or 'Frisee de Namur'.

LETTUCE – grow in unheated or frost-free greenhouse or cold frame, most will be ready to cut April/May; varieties 'Kellys' (crisphead, sow November to January), 'Plus' (butterhead, sow November). Outdoors – sow in autumn and protect with cloches; variety 'Valdor'.

ONIONS – over-wintering varieties can occupy the ground from autumn till June and provide good quality onions when normal maincrop onions are in short supply. Use them before starting the new season's main onions.

SAVOY – grow 'Spivoy' like 'Hispi' cabbage, sow in autumn and plant under cloches for spring use; plant the most frost-resistant varieties that mature in winter – most will 'hold' several months once ready to cut; 'Wivoy'.

SORREL – normally thought of as a herb, but also useful as a spinach-like vegetable but better flavoured; a perennial plant that dies down in winter unless protected by cloches, and makes new growth in early spring.

SWISS CHARD – if sown in June produces a crop of leaves and stems for use in summer, dies down in winter and produces a second crop in March and April until plants run to seed.

Chapter 2

Fruit

Not so long ago fruit was only grown seriously in large gardens. But now, thanks to modern research, new techniques and plant breeding, all sorts of tree, bush and cane fruit, as well as strawberries, can be grown quite successfully on a small scale. And as well as the more familiar varieties, there are now lots of different kinds of fruit readily available in nurseries and garden centres. These include unusual kinds such as blueberries that were until recently rarely grown and consequently almost impossible to obtain, and completely new kinds like the Tayberry that have only recently been bred. So the choice has never been wider.

With tree fruit, such as apples and pears, the most significant change has been brought about by the development of highly dwarfing rootstocks. (All fruit trees are grafted on to the roots of another closely related variety to produce a plant with the best characteristics of each – efficient and tolerant roots at one end, and the fruits of your choice at the other.) Whereas fruit trees previously needed a lot of room, those grown on dwarfing rootstocks stay small enough to be planted very close together – or even in pots. This makes it practical to grow several trees in a small garden; a very good idea when it comes to pollination, as many tree fruit need another variety nearby to ensure both set fruit. If you only have room for one tree, 'family' trees allow you to grow several different varieties grafted on to one trunk, so again, they all get pollinated – and you get a selection of apples instead of all the same kind from your tree. Family trees can also be grown on dwarfing rootstocks to give you the best of both worlds. And, as a useful bonus, fruit trees on dwarfing rootstocks start cropping very much sooner than large trees – within a year or two of planting, as against six to eight years.

To make tree fruit even more interesting for small gardens, plant breeding has also come up with quite a few totally new varieties, particularly where apples are concerned. Now it is possible to grow Cox-like fruit in localities where the old favourite would not grow well, as well as a whole new range of tastes and textures. Soft fruit, too, is now available in a lot of new varieties. You can get more compact plants suitable for closer spacing, or which produce heavier or earlier crops. And there are now late-flowering varieties which get round the problem of frost-damaged blossom which might otherwise have prevented you getting a crop. Better still, now that there is such a demand for intensively grown fruit, more nurseries have begun offering cordon-, espalier- and fan-trained trees and bushes, so you don't have to train them yourself – a relatively skilled and long-term undertaking.

Amongst cane fruit such as blackberries and loganberries, totally new hybrids like the Tayberry have been bred. These are designed to produce heavier crops, over a longer period, or with better flavour or a wider range of uses than the original parents. The last few years have also seen the arrival of new and better varieties of 'perpetual' strawberries and autumn-fruiting raspberries – both of which are useful and easy ways of producing popular fruit crops outside their normal season, when they are most expensive in the shops.

But one of the most interesting of the new developments is the way the revival in fruit growing has encouraged all sorts of relatively unusual fruiting plants to appear on sale – things like blueberries, cranberries and even less commonly found plants like Japanese Wineberries. Many of these are attractive enough to be grown in the ornamental garden along with shrubs, even if you don't have a separate area for growing edible crops. Besides these, a good many exotic fruits are now commonly appearing on sale, such as citrus, figs, etc. These and many other commoner 'dwarfed' fruits lend themselves admirably to growing in containers on patios. But quite apart from the way all these new developments have enabled small gardens to become so highly productive, there is another big benefit – they have helped make small gardens very much more interesting to be in. Besides introducing a whole new range of plants, they mean you can now have the fun of watching the almost daily progress of fruit crops developing, whilst looking forward to eating them later.

Planning and Organising the Small Fruit Garden

GROWING CONDITIONS

If you want a productive fruit garden, one of the most important considerations is the site – is your garden really suitable for fruit in the first place? To do well, fruit needs a reasonably sheltered, sunny spot, with fertile soil which is very slightly acid, and good drainage. If your garden does not naturally provide perfect conditions, there are, however, some things you can do to improve them, as we'll see shortly.

Soil

You need a good depth of fertile and well-drained soil to grow fruit – at least 1 ft 6 ins (45 cm) deep for bush and cane fruit, 2 ft (60 cm) deep for most tree fruits, and 3 ft (90 cm) in the case of cherries. The best way to tell what your soil is like, is to dig a hole. This is the only way to see what depth of good soil you have before reaching solid clay or a hard 'pan' or stony layer. Leave the hole for a few days and see how much of it fills with water seeping in from surrounding soil. This shows if you have a high 'water-table', which is as effective a barrier to root penetration as a hard 'pan'. Then fill the hole with water and see how fast it runs away – this shows how good or bad the drainage is.

To check out your soil type, look to see if puddles lie on the surface for long or if the ground dries out like rock or is covered in cracks during summer – these factors indicate heavy clay soils. If the soil appears pale coloured or sandy in texture, and rainwater runs away very fast leaving the surface dry within an hour or two after rain, this indicates a very light, sandy soil. Both types of soil can be improved a great deal by digging in lots of well-rotted organic matter such as manure, garden compost, spent mushroom compost or peat. But with very heavy or very sandy soils, this needs to be done regularly over several years until sufficient improvement is made. (You could use the ground for vegetables and short-term fruit like strawberries for a few years before planting fruit trees and bushes, while you work on improving the soil.)

If the soil is very acid, the pH may be altered by liming, but it is a good idea to find the extent of the problem by having a soil test done rather than rely on trial and error. Soil-test kits are also

31

available in garden centres for DIY use. If the soil is neutral, fruit will still grow well, but on very chalky or alkaline soil plants will tend to produce similar symptoms to Rhododendrons grown under such circumstances – leaves will turn yellow, be stunted and fall off. You can improve the soil by adding moss peat to make it more acid, but you will need to put more round the plant every year as a mulch, and feed it annually with sequestered iron to correct the deficiencies produced by the soil 'locking up' some of the essential mineral nutrients.

Aspect

It is particularly important to shelter fruit from strong winds in spring when the blossom is out, or the petals may be blown off before pollination takes place. Small gardens often provide naturally sheltered sites, as they are commonly surrounded by houses and gardens full of mature shrubs, hedges and fences. Otherwise a fence can be put up to provide shelter – the best sort is not a solid fence that often makes wind eddy over the top, but a more open type that allows some wind to pass through, slowing it down on the way.

Frost can produce the same sort of effect as strong winds in spring, resulting in no pollination and consequently no fruit. This is why fruit needs to be planted somewhere the frost is not trapped (what fruit farmers call a frost hollow or frost pocket) – you can usually spot these areas for yourself as on winter mornings they are the last places frost disappears from the grass. Sloping ground is often good for fruit as both surplus water and frost can run off easily. As for light, most fruit does best grown where the plants receive direct sunlight for most of the day, though they will put up with being shaded for up to half the day.

Location

Many kinds of fruit need a climate where the spring weather is not too severe. For this reason a lot of fruit does better in the south of the country, while some kinds are completely unsuitable for growing elsewhere. Peaches, nectarines, almonds, grapes and figs for instance, may be grown outdoors in the south, but in the north will normally need to be grown under glass. Some kinds of apples, such as Cox, also do best in the south.

Coping with non-ideal Conditions

If your garden does not provide good conditions for fruit growing and cannot conveniently be improved by normal cultivation, it is better to get round the problems some other way rather than struggle to grow things that will never grow – or crop – well. You can, for instance, overcome a lot of problems due to poor or badly drained soil, by growing fruit in pots. This is also a useful technique if you have excessively acid or alkaline acid soil. On very acid soil (Rhododendron country), however, blueberries and cranberries will thrive in the garden. If you live in a frost hollow or in the north of the country, it is a good idea to stick to naturally late-flowering varieties or specially bred late-flowering or frost-proof varieties (these tend to be newer varieties).

LATE-FLOWERING/FROST-PROOF VARIETIES (suitable for growing in frosty areas and in the north)

APPLES, EATING – 'Discovery', 'Egremont Russett', 'Epicure', 'Fortune', 'Greensleeves', 'James Grieve', 'Jester', 'Katy', 'Lord Lambourne', 'Red Ellison', 'Redsleeves', 'Suntan', 'Tydemans Late Orange'.
APPLES, COOKING – 'Howgate Wonder', 'Lane's Prince Albert'.
BLACKBERRIES – all.
BLACKCURRANTS – 'Ben Sarek', 'Ben More', 'Jet', 'Ben Nevis'.
HYBRID BERRIES – all.
RASPBERRIES – all.
PEARS – 'Conference', 'Winter Nellis'.
PLUMS – 'Dennistons Superb' (Gage).
STRAWBERRY – 'Troubador'.

Otherwise grow fruit in pots and keep the plants in a cold greenhouse till after the worst of the cold weather is over, (but being certain to open the door during the day so pollinating insects can find their way in). In a cold or windy site, growing trained fruit on walls makes it easier to protect fruit blossom in the spring – and the developing fruit buds, later on when the crop is ripening – because you can easily drop nets down over the plants when needed. (Secure a batten to the wall above the plants and tack the netting to it or put in hooks for temporary netting.) The wall will itself offer quite a bit of protection, by retaining heat – the net should then be sufficient to keep off harmful levels of frost, and also give some shelter from wind. On north-facing walls, fan-trained Morello cherries and cordon-trained red-currants, and gooseberries will all grow and crop well. For permanently slightly shaded areas, alpine strawberries, Goose-berry 'Whinham's Industry', whitecurrants and blackberries are the best choice; on poor soil blackberries and Raspberry 'Malling Promise' will thrive; and in wet soil blackcurrants and cran-berries do well and, provided it is not waterlogged, gooseberries will tolerate it.

Access

This last consideration is a purely practical one. Fruit needs to be easily get-at-able by you for such operations as spraying, picking and cultivating – but not too accessible to people outside the garden, or you'll find other people will benefit from your crops of fruit more than you do!

FITTING FRUIT INTO A SMALL SPACE

Growing fruit in small gardens is something of a compromise between finding the place that offers the best growing conditions, and the one where fruit fits in best with the design and layout of the garden.

Walls are an obvious choice. Not only do they provide good sheltered growing conditions for fruit, enabling you to get a lot of productivity without taking up any garden space at all; walls also look most attractive covered with trained fruit trees and bushes. Fan-, cordon- or espalier-trained kinds can be grown not only beside garden walls and fences, but also against the walls of a shed, garage or even the house itself.

If you normally keep part of the garden specially for growing vegetables, you could use cordon-trained or cane fruit as a screen, separating it from the rest of the garden. The plants will then need some means of support – either posts and wires, trellis or wire netting, with the main stems of cordon plants tied on to canes. This looks quite ornamental.

Blackberries and hybrid berries also look most attractive grown over an arch; this is also a convenient way of keeping the plants tidy, as well as restricting them to a limited space.

You can also grow some fruit as a hedge. Soft fruit, such as blackcurrants, can be planted at closer-than-usual spacing to form a continuous row, and apples can be grown as inclined cordons spaced close together in a row, or as horizontal cordons to form a low edging to a lawn or perhaps round a vegetable bed. Strawberries can be fitted in to almost any of these schemes as ground cover amongst other fruit. Although, in theory, fruit is normally best grown with bare soil between the plants, provided you feed more than usual, neither the strawberries nor the fruit they grow round appear any the worse.

You can also grow some of the more unusual or decorative fruit in amongst ornamental plants in mixed borders. Some such as mulberries, Japanese wineberry, etc. do not produce a particularly heavy crop but since they have plenty of ornamental value, can be regarded as dual-purpose plants offering two benefits from the space of one plant.

But the most intensive way of growing fruit is in pots. This way, besides being able to improve on poor growing conditions that may exist in the garden soil, you can move plants about easily – from greenhouse to garden, or from shade into sun during the day if need be, as well as being able to pack an awful lot of plants into a small space and making them look nice. Growing fruit in pots naturally tends to keep the plants smaller than usual, and provided the containers are big enough, any fruit (except raspberries) can be grown in this way. Strawberries can even be grown in windowboxes, if you are really short of space.

Other Planning Considerations

But apart from what you can grow and how you can find room for it, it is also important to take into account what fruit you are likely to use most of, and in what sort of quantities; whether you have a freezer to store surplus crops; whether a single plant will pollinate itself or you need to plant two to ensure getting a crop; what sort of workload you are taking on; and how long you will have to wait for results.

MAKING USE OF THE HARVEST

Obviously it makes sense to grow more of what the family like best – and of those kinds, more of the varieties that allow you to freeze them, convert them to jam or otherwise preserve them to use out of season, as there is only so much you can use fresh.

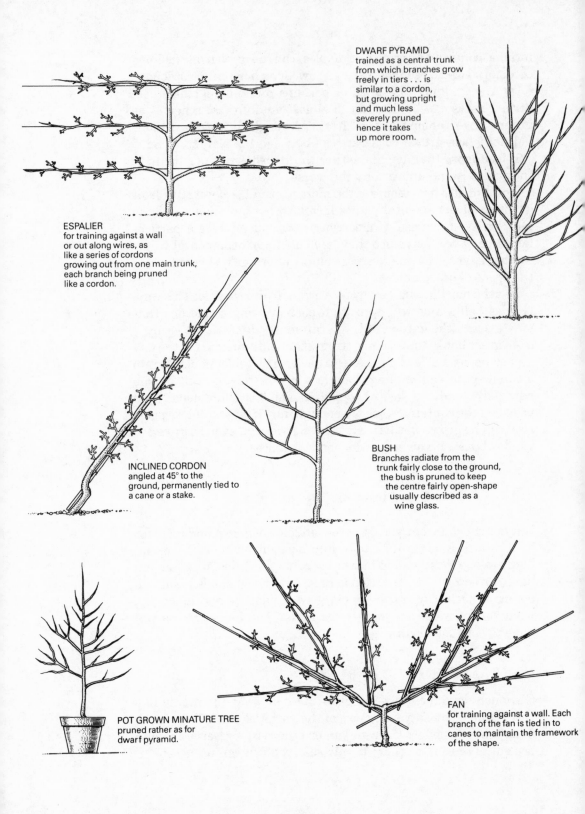

DWARF PYRAMID
trained as a central trunk
from which branches grow
freely in tiers . . . is
similar to a cordon,
but growing upright
and much less
severely pruned
hence it takes
up more room.

ESPALIER
for training against a wall
or out along wires, as
like a series of cordons
growing out from one main trunk,
each branch being pruned
like a cordon.

INCLINED CORDON
angled at 45° to the
ground, permanently tied to
a cane or a stake.

BUSH
Branches radiate from the
trunk fairly close to the ground,
the bush is pruned to keep
the centre fairly open-shape
usually described as a
wine glass.

POT GROWN MINATURE TREE
pruned rather as for
dwarf pyramid.

FAN
for training against a wall. Each
branch of the fan is tied in to
canes to maintain the framework
of the shape.

Fruit for Freezing

Fruit is never quite the same when it comes out of the freezer as it was when it went in; it is best used for cooking rather than trying to pass it off as fresh. However, freezing is a good way of storing surplus crops for out of season use. Any fruit can be frozen, but some varieties are specially recommended:

BLACKBERRIES – 'Bedford Giant', 'Ashton Cross', 'Marion'.

BLACKCURRANTS – 'Jet', 'Ben Lomond'.

BLUEBERRIES AND CRANBERRIES – any.

GOOSEBERRIES – 'Invicta', 'Jubilee'.

HYBRID BERRIES – Tayberry, Tummelberry, Thornless Youngberry.

PEARS – 'Doyenne du Comice', 'Williams Bon Chretien'.

PLUMS – 'Warwickshire Drooper'.

RASPBERRIES – 'Malling Jewel', 'Leo', 'Glen Moy', 'Glen Prosen', 'Malling Joy', 'Sceptre', 'Fallgold' (yellow-fruited).

REDCURRANTS – any.

STRAWBERRIES – 'Totem', 'Shuksan', 'Tyee'.

Other Means of Preserving

Virtually all fruit can be made into jams, jellies or home-made wine; bottling is still done though less so than before the advent of domestic freezers. But if you have surplus crops that you don't want to freeze it is often useful to have a few extra ideas for ways of using them.

HERB JELLIES – Mint or thyme jelly are good ways of using surplus apples; make apple jelly and add the appropriate herb when the fruit is boiled.

FRUIT IN BRANDY – a nice way of turning 'special' fruit, such as peaches or mulberries, into a preserve that can then be used as a dessert – specially nice with ice-cream.

RUM POT – for preserving soft fruit, which are added in layers to a jar and topped up with rum (or brandy) to cover each new layer of fruit. Again, good with ice-cream.

Jam-making

The following varieties are specially recommended for jam-making:

BLACKBERRY – 'Ashton Cross'.

BLACKCURRANTS – 'Jet'.

BLUEBERRY – any.
GOOSEBERRY – 'Invicta' (also bottles specially well), 'Leveller'.
JAPANESE WINEBERRY.
PLUMS – 'Pershore Yellow', 'Laxtons Cropper'.
RASPBERRY – 'Malling Promise'.
STRAWBERRY – 'Tantallon', 'Headley', 'Cambridge Favourite', 'Saladin', 'Troubador'.
TUMMELBERRY.

POLLINATION

It is also essential to make sure the crops you grow will be properly pollinated, or you'll either get no crop at all, or at best only part of what you should be entitled to. Soft fruit are self-fertile which means a single bush, or a row of canes or strawberries all of the same variety, will produce a good crop. If you grow blueberries, you are recommended to grow two different varieties together to get the best crop, although each is technically self-fertile.

With tree fruit the situation is a little more complicated – though not half as complicated as it is sometimes made to sound. The problem is that many tree fruits, notably apples, pears and cherries, are not self-fertile so they have to be cross-pollinated in order to set fruit. This, clearly, can't happen unless both varieties flower at the same time, and the purpose of pollination charts is to group together those varieties that do just that, so you can easily see which will pollinate each other. What complicates things is that some varieties, known as triploids, not only won't pollinate themselves, but also they won't pollinate any other apples either. So if you grow a triploid variety you need to plant *two* other varieties with it – all of which flower at the same time – so they pollinate the triploid *and* each other.

Of course, you may get away without planting more than one tree. If you have neighbours who grow similar kinds of fruit to yourself, provided they have suitable pollinators, you should get a good crop. The ornamental crab-apples 'Golden Hornet' and 'John Downie', will also pollinate domestic apples. But bees won't travel far so unless pollinators are fairly close by it is safer to plant one of your own – within 100 yards/metres at most. Otherwise you can get round the problem by growing a 'family' tree – three different varieties that cross-pollinate each other, all grafted on to the same trunk – or grow one of the few self-fertile varieties.

Pollination Guide – Tree Fruit

Any of the following varieties will cross-pollinate each other – only a selection of better-known varieties are shown; triploid varieties are marked with a 'T'.

APPLES

'Blenheim Orange' (T)	'Bramley's Seedling'	'Cox's Orange Pippin'	'Crispin' (T)
'Discovery'	'Epicure'	'Fiesta'	'Fortune'
'Greensleeves'	'Golden Delicious'	'James Grieve'	'Jester'
'Jupiter' (T)	'Katy'	'Kent'	'Queen Cox'
'Sunset'	'Suntan' (T)	'Redsleeves'	'Worcester Pearmain'

'Spartan' and 'Idared' won't cross-pollinate each other, but both are pollinated by the group shown above. All are also pollinated by crab-apples 'John Downie' and 'Golden Hornet'.

Self-fertile – 'Greensleeves', 'Winston'.

CHERRY

'Merchant'   'Early Rivers'   'Merton Glory'

Self-fertile – 'Stella', 'Morello' (cooking cherry).

PEACHES, NECTARINES, ALMONDS

Self-fertile – all varieties.

PEARS

'Beth'	'Doyenne du Comice'	'Conference'
'Beurre Hardy'	'Williams Bon Chretien'	

Self-fertile – 'Durondeau'.

PLUMS

Self-fertile – 'Czar', 'Laxtons Cropper', 'Marjories Seedling', Purple Pershore', 'Victoria', 'Warwickshire Drooper'.

WORKLOAD

If time is tight, an extra factor that needs taking into account is the amount of work it takes to grow fruit in a small garden.

There's no doubt about it, the more intensively you cultivate fruit, the more work is involved. This is specially so in the case of highly trained forms such as fans and cordons which need pruning properly in both summer and winter, and pot-grown fruit which needs regular and frequent watering in summer. Most fruit will also need protecting from birds; if you are to enjoy the results of your efforts it is a good idea to cover plants with nets while the crop is developing and ripening. On the plus side, however, two of the most time-consuming and fiddly jobs connected with large-scale fruit growing – spraying and pruning – are much more quickly and easily done when you grow highly trained, compact forms like cordons and fans, because you can reach without having to stand on a ladder, and there is also a lot less plant to prune.

Let's now look at the routine jobs and how they apply to small gardens in more detail.

Spraying

If you want to do the job properly, a full spraying programme for fruit can involve nine or ten sprays over the season. But lots of people nowadays prefer not to use any more chemical sprays than is absolutely necessary on things they are going to eat, and plenty more just do not have time to do so much spraying. Fortunately, in a small garden you can cut down quite considerably. Rather than follow a proper spray programme, a much better policy is to spray routinely *only* to prevent the sort of pests like maggots that are going to make your fruit unpleasant to eat – and beyond that, only spray when you actually find that you have a problem, like greenfly. One thing that is worth doing even if you use no other spray at all, is giving a winter wash spray with tar oil, as this takes care of a lot of over-wintering grubs etc. besides giving the plants a good pre-spring clean-up.

Pruning

Again, this is an aspect of fruit growing that often appears intimidatingly complex. Basically, the reason for pruning is to keep compact, trained plants small and neat instead of letting them slowly become overgrown when they take up more room. It also helps keep them as productive as possible by encouraging the

Successful plant combination – tall ornamental grass, variegated ivy
and yellow flowered euphorbia.

Productive small garden with a bit of everything, flowers, shrubs, a few fruit trees and vegetables, greenhouse, shed and lawn.

sort of growth that produces fruit rather than just lots of leaves and more stems.

Whereas normal bush-grown soft or tree fruit can just have the oldest stems removed completely each winter to open up the centre and leave well-spaced-out shoots behind, with cordon- or fan-trained plants the job needs more precision. The main 'compact' training systems are shown in the diagram.

Netting

In a small garden where you only have room to grow enough fruit for yourself without allowing for losses, it is virtually essential to protect soft fruits and the softer tree fruits from birds. Birds will take fruit long before it is ripe enough for our liking, and you can lose an entire crop before getting a look in. Special fruit cages are available, and in country areas where birds are a real problem, they are probably worthwhile. But they take up a lot of room, and are not terribly practical if you have fruit dotted all round the garden. Fruit grown on walls, and compact free-standing trees can, however, be draped with netting quite easily. Better still, construct some sort of frame out of canes which will hold the net at least a beak's-length clear of the crop.

Cultivations

Highly trained fruit, especially trees on very dwarfing rootstocks, will do very much better if you grow them in bare soil which is kept regularly weeded, rather than growing them surrounded by grass. Apples on M27, the most dwarfing of all rootstocks, should *only* be grown in bare soil. Hoeing should be done as shallowly as possible to avoid disturbing or cutting through small surface roots. Strawberries can be grown for ground cover beneath fan-trained trees or cordons if you wish, provided the plants are given extra feeding and watering to compensate for the competition. Alpine strawberries are specially useful grown this way as they do well in the shade.

A Typical Year's Calendar of Essential Routine Work

APRIL – Start hoeing shallowly between fruit; mulch with well-rotted organic matter such as compost or manure to retain moisture and suppress weeds.

MAY – Spray apples against sawfly (maggots) with systemic insecticide one week after petals fall. Put up nets to protect developing fruit from birds as soon as flowers are over.

JUNE – Spray raspberries, blackberries and hybrid berries every week against raspberry beetle (maggots) with derris as soon as the flowers start to open. Spray apples against codling moth (maggots) with a systemic insecticide.

JULY – Continue spraying cane fruit against raspberry beetle every week while the flowers are open. Summer prune cordon-, espalier- and fan-trained fruit. Leave this till late in the month in the north.

AUGUST – Cut out old raspberry canes after all the fruit has been picked. Tie current year's shoots into position.

OCTOBER – Cut out old-fruited canes from blackberries and hybrid berries. Tie current year's shoots into position. Plant new strawberry plants if required.

NOVEMBER TO EARLY MARCH – Winter prune fruit trees and bushes. Spray with tar wash. Plant new fruit trees, bushes and canes (except in frosty weather or when the ground is very wet); prune immediately after planting.

How Long do you have to Wait?

In small gardens, fast results are often an important factor in deciding what fruit to plant. Fortunately, modern dwarfing rootstocks have considerably speeded up the time taken for tree fruits to start cropping. Whereas you would have had to wait six to eight years for a reasonable crop of apples from an old-fashioned fruit tree, you can now expect it to take only two or three years – so you will be picking something probably the same year as you plant. Pears take rather longer to start cropping, perhaps three or four years; plums and cherries about the same. Soft fruit, including both canes and bushes, are faster and will be producing quite well in their second year after planting. The fastest crops are to be had from strawberries, which from a November planting will produce a good crop in their first summer, and annual fruits grown from seed, such as melons, Cape gooseberries and huckleberries.

Varieties

DWARFING ROOTSTOCKS FOR FRUIT TREES

Before the days of dwarfing rootstocks it was difficult, if not impossible, to grow fruit trees in small gardens – if you wanted to leave room for anything else as well. But now dwarfing rootstocks are commonly used, and all sorts of very restricted training systems such as cordons are available besides making it possible to grow miniature fruit trees in pots. Rootstocks vary in the degree of dwarfing effect they produce, and some are more suited than others to particular types of training systems and soil types. As a general rule, the more dwarfing the effect, the sooner they start cropping, the better the soil they need, and the better they need to be looked after to produce good results – but the smaller the total crop per plant will be. To make up for the smaller crop you can, however, plant very much more intensively than usual.

APPLE M27 – the most dwarfing rootstock, used for trees grown in pots or for miniature cordons in very good soil only – it is essential to keep the soil round the trees free from weeds. Plants grown in open ground have such small root systems they need to be permanently tied to a stake. Trees reach a maximum height of about 5–7 ft (1.5–2.1 m), and when plants are in full crop, you should get 15–20 lbs (7–9 kg) of fruit per tree. Plant mini-cordons 18 ins (45 cm) apart, or grow as miniature trees in 15–18 in. (37.5–45 cm) pots.

APPLE M9 – very dwarfing in effect; used for cordons, dwarf pyramids and small bush trees, it produces a tree 6–8 ft (1.8–2.4 m) high, which will still need permanent staking but gives approximately 40 lbs (18 kg) of fruit when in full production. Needs reasonably good soil. Space cordons 2 ft 6 ins (75 cm) apart, dwarf pyramids 5 ft (1.5 m) apart, bush trees 7–8 ft (2.1–2.4 m) apart and espaliers 10 ft (3 m) apart.

APPLE M26 – semi-dwarfing; used for slightly less-restrictive training systems like espaliers, dwarf pyramids, and fans as well as small bush trees, but also suitable for cordons on poor or dry soil where growth is naturally less vigorous. Grows trees 8–10 ft (2.4–3 m) high. Space cordons 2 ft 6 ins (75 cm) apart, espaliers 10–12 ft (3–3.6 m) apart and other forms 6 ft (1.8 m) apart.

PEAR – Quince C is the most dwarfing of the pear rootstocks, though it produces a rather larger tree than the dwarfing apple stocks, from 10–16 ft (3–4.8 m) depending on your soil type. It is used for cordons, espaliers, bush and dwarf pyramid trees, and can be expected to take a year or two longer for trees to start cropping than apples grafted on very dwarfing rootstocks. Plant cordons 2 ft 6 ins (75 cm) apart, and other forms 12–15 ft (3.6–4.5 m apart.

CHERRY – Colt was the first generally available dwarfing rootstock for cherries, which are normally very vigorous trees that would be quite unsuitable for small gardens. It is nevertheless only a semi-dwarfing rootstock, restricting trees to about half their normal size – they can, however, be kept to about 10–12 ft (3–3.6 m) by pruning. Cropping should start in the third or fourth year. Use Colt for fans and small bush trees; space 12–15 ft (3.6–4.5 m) apart. But there's an even newer cherry rootstock being offered now – GM9 – and it is so dwarfing that you can grow it in a pot.

PLUM – Pixy rootstock gives you a plum tree that grows only about 10 ft (3 m) high, which is used for fans, dwarf pyramids or small bush trees and spaced 10–12 ft (3–3.6 m) apart. Expect trees grown on Pixy to start cropping well in their fourth year from planting.

PEACH, NECTARINE – St Julian A is the most dwarfing rootstock currently available, though several potential new rootstocks are being tried experimentally that should produce more dwarfing effect. St Julian A is used for small bushes and fans; space plants 12–15 ft (3.6–4.5 m) apart. They should start cropping in the fourth or fifth year after planting.

SPECIALLY PRODUCTIVE OR SPACE-SAVING VARIETIES

Tree Fruit

A lot of new fruit-tree varieties have recently been produced by the research organisations who breed new varieties for the commercial grower; many of these are very suitable for the amateur gardener too and are available through various mail-order nurserymen. Generally the new varieties offer significant benefits over old ones in terms of things like heavy cropping, or ease of growing. With apples, for instance, the old favourite 'Cox's Orange Pippin' does not grow happily in the north of the country or where growing conditions are not ideal, and produces a relatively light crop at the best of times; now new varieties have been bred that retain the flavour of Cox, but which are much easier to grow, and produce much heavier crops. Self-fertile varieties, where they exist, are also ideal for small gardens where there is only room for a single tree to be grown.

The following are some of the most interesting new varieties of tree fruit on the market.

APPLES (all eating apples)

'CRISPIN' – pick in October; keeps well. Large yellowish-greenish apples, good flavour, juicy texture.

'FIESTA' – Cox taste and appearance, but easier to grow and a much heavier cropper. Pick September and October; stores well. Good flavour, crisp texture.

'GREENSLEEVES' – pick late September; does not keep long. Looks like a Golden Delicious, but much better flavour. Very heavy cropper. Self-fertile so can be grown on its own away from other apples.

'IDARED' – pick end October; keeps well. Striking red-flushed yellow apples often seen in the shops; dual-purpose variety used for cooking as well as eating.

'JESTER' – pick September to November; red and yellow fruit; good flavour and crisp texture.

'JONAGOLD' – pick October; keeps well. Large yellow apples, good flavour.

'JUPITER' – pick in October; keeps very well. Cox-like taste and appearance; exceptionally heavy cropper.

'KATY' – early variety for picking September and October; good flavour, crisp texture. Scarlet-flushed fruit.

'KENT' – like an improved Golden Delicious; best kept for a few months before eating.

'REDSLEEVES' – early variety; very heavy cropper; bright red fruit with sweet flavour and juicy texture.

'SPARTAN' – pick October; keeps well. Dark red apples; very good sweet flavour, juicy texture.

'SUNSET' – pick end October; keeps well. Cox-like taste and appearance, but heavier cropping and much easier to grow; crisp texture.

45

'SUNTAN' – pick in October; keeps well. Large Cox-type apples, very good flavour. Particularly recommended for areas prone to late frosts.

PEARS
'BETH' – an early dessert variety to pick in September and October, though it will keep for a month or two. Exceptionally heavy cropper.

CHERRIES
'STELLA' – the first self-fertile sweet cherry. Grafted on Colt rootstock this produces a tree which makes it possible to grow a single, small cherry tree conveniently in a small garden. Stella is also occasionally available grafted on to the newer and even more dwarfing rootstock GM9 which makes a small tree suitable for growing in a pot.

Soft Fruit

Here again, work done for commercial growers has had a big spin-off for amateurs. Many new varieties now exist that produce heavier crops, greater frost resistance (particularly amongst the new blackcurrants), disease resistance, more compact plants, or more useful still, the capability for out-of-season production, as for instance with autumn-fruited raspberries and the so-called perpetual-fruited strawberries.

The following are some of the most useful new varieties to look out for.

BLACKCURRANTS
The biggest improvement from blackcurrant breeding has been to produce varieties that flower later so as to avoid flowers being damaged by frost and not pollinated. This means blackcurrants are now much more suited to growing in the north of the country and in low-lying areas subject to frost. As a plus, these new varieties are heavier croppers than the old favourites. Varieties with late flowers for frost resistance include 'Ben Sarek', 'Ben More', 'Ben Lomond', 'Jet' and 'Ben Nevis'. Of these, 'Ben Sarek' is particularly suited to small gardens as it is very compact, only growing about 3 ft–3 ft 6 ins (90–105 cm) high. Plants can be spaced slightly closer together than usual; it's also a good variety for growing in pots, and produces one of the highest yields of any blackcurrant variety.

REDCURRANTS

Not so much work has been done here, probably because they are a less important crop commercially. The new variety 'Stanza', however, is a heavy cropper which flowers late and thus avoids frost which could otherwise prevent it from cropping well in northern districts.

GOOSEBERRY

New varieties of gooseberry are bred for heavy crops and disease resistance – they are still working on the problem of a thornless goosegog, and are very nearly there! Best of the new varieties for small gardens is 'Invicta', an exceptionally heavy cropper producing something like double the crops of old varieties. Good for cooking, freezing and bottling, it is mildew resistant – but very thorny indeed, though as it is an upright bush picking is marginally easier, especially on cordon-trained plants. 'Jubilee' is a very heavy cropper whose fruit can be used green or left on the plant to ripen for dessert use; 'Captivator' is a nearly spineless variety with red fruit.

BLACKBERRY

Blackberries are not normally recommended for small gardens as they take up so much room and are inhospitably prickly. But by choosing a compact variety and training it round a fence, you have a productive vandal- and intruder-proof barrier – or you can select one of the thornless varieties for easy picking.

Particularly interesting varieties are the 'Merton Thornless' blackberry, a compact thornless variety with 1 in. (25 mm) diameter fruit; 'Ashton Cross', not particularly compact but an exceptionally heavy cropper; and 'Fantasia', one of the newest varieties with not only heavy crops but also exceptionally large fruit, the size of a 10p coin.

HYBRID BERRIES

Relatives of the blackberry, these hybrids include loganberry, Tayberry and newly bred hybrids, all having large scrambling canes similar to blackberries, with loganberry-like fruit. New varieties are generally bred to have longer picking seasons and for a wider range of culinary purposes than either blackberry or loganberry. Of particular interest in small gardens are: Tayberry, a cross between blackberry and raspberry, much like a loganberry, with large purple fruit; Tummelberry, a Tayberry cross

47

with reddish fruit – a very heavy cropper for eating fresh, cooking, freezing or jam-making; Marionberry (now considered to be a blackberry variety called Marion), large berries with very good flavour and an unusually long cropping period (mid July to late September) – its fruit can be used fresh, cooked or frozen; Silvanberry, the newest hybrid, from Australia, which is a very heavy cropper with good quality fruit.

RASPBERRIES

Probably the biggest problem with raspberries is that, after a few years, the canes invariably become affected by virus disease which is spread by aphids; affected plants gradually produce smaller and smaller crops. In a small garden, particularly, this is a terrible waste of space. For this reason it is worth planting new varieties that resist aphids as the plants not only crop better, but also they keep cropping well for longer than other raspberries; look for 'Glen Moy' (which is also virtually spineless for more comfortable picking), 'Malling Delight', 'Glen Prosen', 'Malling Joy' (resistant to four different kinds of aphid so likely to remain virus-free more reliably than most), and 'Leo'.

Standard varieties of raspberry produce a crop in mid to late summer, just after the strawberry season is over. But you can produce out-of-season crops easily by growing autumn-fruiting raspberries. These crop from late August until the start of the frosts. But besides producing a crop when raspberries are not normally available, the autumn-fruiting kinds are specially suitable for small gardens as they do not need a permanent support system like normal raspberries. The autumn-fruited kinds are much shorter so they don't need tying up. Their canes grow during the summer, fruit in the autumn and are cut down to ground level in late February. Varieties include 'Autumn Bliss', 'Sceptre', 'September', 'Zeva', 'Heritage' and 'Fallgold', a yellow-fruited autumn raspberry.

STRAWBERRIES

Of the standard strawberry varieties, the old favourite 'Royal Sovereign' is not grown so much now as it is prone to mildew, and only carries light crops. Some of the new varieties, on the other hand, are particularly heavy croppers – especially 'Harvester', 'Bounty', 'Grandee', 'Pantagruella' and 'Tamella'.

You can also use 'perpetual-fruiting' strawberries to extend the cropping season. Unlike 'normal' strawberries, which only crop

over a short period around midsummer, perpetual-fruiting strawberries crop continuously over the whole summer and autumn.
This is not quite as good as it sounds though, because the amount
of fruit you can pick at any one time tends to be rather less than
you would pick from normal varieties, and it is often produced in
short 'flushes'. In practice the best way of treating perpetual
strawberries is to use them for autumn cropping, and use a
normal variety to produce the midsummer crop. To get the
maximum autumn production from perpetual strawberries,
remove their flowers in spring, up till late May, so all their
energies are diverted into a single burst. And to make the most of
the autumn strawberry season, cover the plants with cloches
when the weather starts to get cold around late September.

The newer varieties of perpetual-fruiting strawberries are
generally heavier croppers than the first ones that appeared on
the market. Specially good ones include 'Rapella', 'Rabunda' and
'Ostara'.

An even more exciting development are 'daylength neutral'
strawberry varieties. Whereas normal strawberries are 'trig-
gered' to fruit by the right number of daylight hours, these
varieties are completely unaffected by daylength, and will crop
whenever the temperature is over 50°F (10°C). This means they
can be grown in pots and kept under glass or on a sunny
windowsill indoors to crop during the winter or early spring, then
be moved out into the garden in summer, and brought back under
cover to continue cropping in the autumn. As you might expect,
after a year of continuous cropping the plants are not much good
for further use, and it is best to replace them with new ones. The
original plants need not be wasted though; they can be planted
out in the garden and used as normal summer strawberries
afterwards.

Varieties include 'Fern', 'Douglas' and 'Selva'. 'Douglas' prefers
more warmth than the others and is best suited to growing
permanently under glass.

Special Space Saving Growing Techniques

GROWING IN POTS

Growing fruit in pots is specially useful where space is short as it
allows you to take advantage of any level hard surfaces such as

patios and paths, so long as they are in a sunny and sheltered spot.

Any fruit, except raspberries, can be grown in containers – provided you use large enough containers. In most cases, fruit that can be grown indefinitely in a pot 15–18 ins (37.5–45 cm) in diameter are most suitable as they are not too difficult to move about when necessary. To grow fruit in pots, as a general rule, the plants are treated almost exactly the same as you would grow any patio pot plant when it comes to feeding and watering. The only difference is that you need to prune them properly, but you do this just as you would if the same tree or bush was growing in the garden.

In summer, you will find container-grown fruit needs much more water than you would expect – the pots will be filled completely with roots and consequently dry out very quickly indeed. In hot, sunny weather you may need to water twice a day. This is particularly important with fruit, as otherwise the crop may be shed prematurely. Regular feeding with liquid feed (use the high potash type usually sold for feeding tomatoes) is also essential – feed about once or twice a week using the rate of dilution recommended on the bottle from the time leaves open in spring till they fall in autumn.

In winter the pots need to be 'lagged' with newspaper or sacking, sunk into the garden soil in a well-drained spot, or best of all, moved into a cold greenhouse. This is to protect the roots from excessive freezing, which is necessary as they do not have the protection of surrounding soil as they would planted in the garden.

Tree Fruit

The best forms for growing in pots are miniature bush trees or cordons. Use only trees grown on the most dwarfing rootstocks available for pot growing (M27 for apples, GM5 for cherries, St Julian A for peaches and nectarines). Pears and plums are not normally recommended for growing in pots, though you might try using the most dwarfing stocks such as Pixy and St Julian A, and rather larger containers.

Bush Fruit

Any bush fruit grow well in 15–18 in. (37.5–45 cm) pots, but where possible, choose the more compact types such as Ben Sarek blackcurrant. Train blackcurrants as bushes, when they will grow rather smaller than the same plant out in the garden. Redcurrants and gooseberries can be trained as small bushes or as double or triple cordons.

Large cane fruit, like loganberries etc., may be grown in large containers if space makes any other means of growing them impossible, but frankly their size and shape makes them rather top-heavy for containers – if you decide to try, use a container of about half a cubic yard (metre) capacity and train the stems out across a wall or fence for support.

Strawberries must be *the* most successful fruit ever for pots. You can plant them in multi-storey 'Towerpots', traditional terracotta strawberry pots with lots of planting holes in the sides, in grow bags, or even in hanging baskets provided you can keep them well enough watered. By growing them in pots, it is then very easy to move strawberry plants under glass to 'force' them for extra early crops – leave them outside for most of the year, but bring them into cold or slightly heated greenhouse, sunny room or cold frame in early January. Make sure the windows are open when the flowers are out so insects can get in to pollinate them (or do it yourself with a small artist's paintbrush), and you'll have fruit for Wimbledon. Specially suitable varieties for forcing are: 'Tantallon', 'Cambridge Vigour' (does particularly well in growing bags), 'Silver Jubilee', 'Cambridge Favourite', and any of the daylength neutral varieties, provided you can keep them heated above 50°F (10°C).

Blueberries and cranberries can also be grown in large pots, but as they dislike lime in their soil be sure to use ericaceous compost rather than the ordinary potting types.

Ornamental Fruit

In a very small garden, or where there is no room to grow fruit in a separate fruit and vegetable garden, you can grow the more ornamental kinds along with other plants in mixed borders. True, many of them do not give enormously high yields, but it can often be nice to include plants that are ornamental as well as useful; a bit like getting two plants in the space of one. Blueberries are good if you have acid soil, as their foliage takes on beautiful red and gold tints in the autumn. Cherry trees on dwarfing rootstocks look good enough to pass as ornamental flowering cherries round about April or May, when fan-trained peaches or nectarines on walls look a picture too. Alpine strawberries grow well in the shade, and make pretty ground-cover plants under trees.

But one of the best fruit to grow in the ornamental garden is Japanese Wineberry. This has very pretty red canes which stand out particularly well in winter when the foliage has fallen. The fruit are orange at first, turning to red when they ripen in August; they can be used for dessert or made into jam.

Another useful fruiting shrub is the mulberry. The black mulberry, *Morus nigra*, is the best for fruit production – get the cultivar Chelsea if you can; the white mulberry is better for feeding to silkworms. Mulberries can take eight years or more to start bearing fruit, but are faster if you grow them in containers when they will crop in about three or four years.

Exotic and/or Unusual Fruit

Many unusual or exotic fruit make good pot plants to grow on a patio in summer, or for the greenhouse. Again, although crops are not huge, the method of production is very intensive so you don't need much room and you also have the advantage of enjoying plants that are both interesting to grow, and productive.

CITRUS FRUITS

Old favourites from Victorian times, citrus fruits are beginning to become available again in a reasonable selection of varieties. They make attractive plants, with their oval-shaped evergreen leaves; grown in a 12–15 in. (30–37.5 cm) pot they can be kept as relatively small bushes about 3–4 ft (90–120 cm) high for years, given a little light pruning. What is particularly fascinating about them is the way you get flowers (which are beautifully scented), immature green fruit, and fully ripe fruit, all on the same plant at the same time. All members of the citrus family need warmth in winter (a heated greenhouse or sunroom, or a windowsill indoors is ideal), but they can be stood out on a sunny, sheltered patio in summer, between June and September.

Lemons are the most readily available citrus plants, and can be found in many good garden centres. The variety 'Meyers Lemon' is probably the best to grow as it produces very large fruit, plenty of them, and tolerates reasonably low winter temperatures – a minimum of 45°F (7°C). Kumquats, those fascinating, miniature, oval-shaped, orange-like fruits, will also do well at the same winter temperature. Limes, and the even more unusual variegated lemon (which has variegated leaves and fruit), pink grape-fruit, jaffa oranges, tangerines, etc. need a winter temperature of 50°F (10°C) or above. These are normally only available from specialist nurserymen.

FIGS

Although figs are often planted outdoors they grow into large plants more suited to big gardens, and it takes a good summer for them to ripen the fruit. If you have a greenhouse or sunroom, it is a much better idea to grow a fig in a large pot. This not only keeps the plants relatively small – a bush about 4 ft (120 cm) high – it makes them enormously productive as every branch is tipped with a cluster of figs. And instead of growing one of the usual outdoor varieties like 'Brown Turkey', get a greenhouse variety from a specialist nursery instead. Kept under glass, any of these will produce the most delicious ripe fruit throughout late summer and early autumn, and you can choose from varieties that have black figs (such as 'Negro Largo'), white figs (such as 'White Marseilles') or even violet figs (such as 'Violette Dauphine'), when the fruit are ripe. If you want to stand them on the patio in summer you can, but they may not crop quite so long or so heavily.

GRAPES

Grapevines can be grown over a pergola or on a trellis over a wall, but generally the varieties that grow best outdoors are only suitable for making into wine. If you want dessert grapes for eating, you need suitable varieties such as 'Black Hamburg', which must be grown under glass. They can be trained up and over the inside of a greenhouse or conservatory (which does not need to be heated), where they look very decorative. But for maximum productivity when space is more limited, vines can also be grown in a 15–18 in. (37.5–45 cm) pot and trained up three canes in a pyramid. This has the advantage of portability if you need to move the plants around, and despite the degree to which the vine is restricted, it produces a surprisingly good crop grown this way.

MELONS

Grown under glass, melons can be one of the most productive of fruit crops. They also taste so much better when they are allowed to ripen fully on the plant – you would scarcely recognise them as the same fruit that you buy in the greengrocers. Musk melons and watermelons need a warmer climate than ours, or a very early start (January) and an awful lot of heat to ripen them. The best sort to grow are cantaloupes, which are small, plentifully produced, reliable and delicious. Of these, the variety 'Sweetheart' is one of the best, not just for taste but for its amazing ability to ripen reliably, even in a cold summer. Grow cantaloupe melons in pots or the border soil just as you would cucumbers, with the important difference that melon flowers must be pollinated or you don't get any melons.

HUCKLEBERRIES

These have only comparatively recently been available in this country, though they are popular in the USA and Canada. They are grown outdoors, and as they are annuals, are a very useful way of producing a large crop of soft fruit in one year – perhaps while you wait for canes and bushes to get into production. Huckleberries are low-growing, compact, bushy plants that look deceptively like their poisonous cousin, woody nightshade, though the fruit of huckleberries are perfectly safe to eat. Leave them on the plant till they are black and soft, and use them for pies or jam. They can be eaten fresh, but they taste very sharp and need lots of sugar. Half a dozen plants are enough for a pie; they crop very heavily.

CAPE GOOSEBERRIES

Though not heavy croppers, these are interesting plants to grow and don't need much room. Closely related to the Chinese lanterns grown in the garden, Cape gooseberries have very similar golden berries hidden inside papery lantern-like husks. Grow them in pots in the greenhouse, and move them on to the patio in summer if you need the space; if you grow them outside permanently the berries won't have ripened by the end of summer. Leave the fruit on the plants till the lanterns dry out and the berries inside are soft, then use them fresh or in pies or jam.

KIWI FRUIT

These, again, are interesting rather than terribly productive. The plants, botanically known as *Actinidia chinensis*, will grow in the garden though they are unlikely to produce fruit unless you grow them under glass. You need separate male and female plants to produce fruit; grow them in large pots or the greenhouse border, where they will need training on wires or netting as they are naturally large climbing plants.

Chapter 3

Trees and Shrubs

Trees and shrubs form the framework that gives shape to a garden, and they also provide much-needed privacy and shelter. Even in a small garden, you can't do without them. But it does require a slightly different approach to grow what are, after all, relatively large plants in a small garden. This is why the varieties you choose and the way you use them will probably vary quite a bit from the traditional idea of tree and shrub gardening.

Take beds for example: in large gardens, trees and shrubs are normally grown in big borders of their own, where you need lots of large spreading varieties to make an impact. This is clearly not practical in small gardens – there just isn't room. What works much better here is to use fewer, compacter-growing shrubs, but to make much more of them. You could, for instance, use a few well-placed trees and shrubs in mixed borders, as the background to colourful herbaceous and annual flowers and bulbs. Or, rather than having traditional borders round the edge of the garden, try growing shrubs in island beds instead – a very good way of showing off a well-chosen group of plants to advantage.

When it comes to choosing varieties for small gardens, it makes sense to go for naturally compact varieties and 'sub-shrubs' (the smaller, less woody members of the shrub tribe), which not only look more in scale with a small garden, they'll also make much less work as you won't constantly be having to cut them back to fit the space available. But you don't have to sacrifice any of the special appeal of trees and shrubs in the process. By selecting your varieties carefully, and including some with more than one season of interest, you can make sure there is always something colourful to admire in the garden all the year round. In fact, one big advantage of having a small garden is that, with fewer plants to buy, you can justify spending that little bit extra on more interesting and unusual shrubs, or the very best forms, instead of

(ABOVE) Successful plant combination – mixture of ornamental herbs
that are also edible (ornamental sages, thymes and rosemary). All need
a hot sunny well sheltered spot with good drainage.

(BELOW) Colourful small water feature with ornamental heron (which
also helps deter real herons from landing and taking the fish).

Thyme lawn – notice how different varieties have been planted in patchwork quilt fashion to produce an interesting Persian carpet effect. Only prostrate varieties have been used.

settling for the 'ordinary' kinds. And by choosing plants that are right for the soil and situation, you'll be sure of having a superb display without wasting space on plants that don't 'earn their keep' or which end up by making a whole crop of problems for you to solve later!

Techniques

CHOOSING THE RIGHT PLANTS

If you are starting from scratch with a new garden, you have a unique opportunity to get everything right, from the start. So before even starting to look at glossy pictures in brochures or visiting a garden centre, it pays to take a few moments to assess the situation.

Firstly, from the plants' point of view. What is the soil, aspect, and climate like? How much light is there – is the bed in sun all day long, half the day; or is it in permanent shade? Is the soil light and excessively free draining, normal, or wet and heavy clay? Is the site sheltered or exposed, in a cold northern or warm southern location? And finally how much room do you have – what sort of height and spread can shrubs reach without overfilling the space allocated to them?

Once you have a good picture of the planting conditions, you can work out roughly how many plants of what shapes and sizes are going to look right for the spot you have in mind – and set out to put names to them.

In choosing plants it is best to have some kind of plan rather than just buying whatever takes your fancy at the time. A group of plants specially chosen to look nice together makes a much more eye-catching feature than an *ad hoc* collection of plants. Basically, to look good, a group of plants needs to include either contrasting or harmonising colours, and a selection of textures, shapes and sizes. And in selecting them, you can use much the same sort of principles you have (probably unconsciously) used many times over when arranging flowers, choosing curtains, carpets and upholstery, or even clothes that match.

Beyond that, you also need to think of planning for a succession of all-year-round interest. Flowers, for instance, are relatively short-lived, and you don't want everything blooming in the same month with nothing to look at the rest of the year. So choose trees and shrubs that flower one after another for a sequence of flowering – and choose a mixture of varieties to provide lots of small 'filler' flowers and fewer large 'special' ones.

Foliage can be small and shape-filling, or large and striking; evergreen or deciduous, and either green, gold, blue, grey or red. If you are planting a mixed border, you may prefer to choose shrubs that are looking their best when your herbaceous plants and bulbs etc. are not – in which case choose early spring/winter flowering shrubs, those with autumn tints or evergreen foliage. And don't forget there are other seasonal features you can 'plan for' too – such as peeling or coloured bark and contorted twigs which you'll only be able to appreciate in winter; autumn tints, fruit and berries; spring catkins etc. Shapes include low and spreading types (typical of ground-cover plants), rounded, flame or column-shaped (particularly found among conifers), or just loosely bushy (as are a great many shrubs). Given good 'plant associations' as they are called, it is possible to produce exceptionally striking results in a small space – and without using a lot of plants.

SOLVING THE PROBLEMS OF AN OVERGROWN SHRUBBERY

Not everyone can start with a blank slate to write on. Often, you take over a garden someone else has planted and have to make the most of what's already there. And if it turns out to be unsuitably planted – or not to your liking – then you have to tackle the problem. If you really don't like what you find, the only answer is to redesign it entirely, getting rid of unsuitable plants and, where possible, moving others to better positions. If you basically like the layout, but find some plants grossly overgrown while others are not doing well as they are planted in unsuitable places, then you can do something less drastic.

Start by assessing the shrubs growing there. Decide what wants taking out, and what can be salvaged by a bit of judicious pruning. Plants to take out are the naturally large ones which are already overgrown – even with hard pruning these will not be much use as hard pruning tends to produce lots of over-vigorous new growth which does not carry flowers.

Those that are not doing well because they have been planted in totally unsuitable conditions, will also have to come out – like Rhododendrons in chalky soil (if they are dwarf varieties move

58

them into pots of ericaceous compost), or shade-loving plants growing in full sun (these can simply be moved to a shadier spot).

Of the plants that are left, you will probably find small shrubs that have been overshadowed by larger ones and in consequence have become drawn up and leggy. These can be improved by pruning them hard back to make them grow bushier. It may mean missing a year's flowering, but in the long run it will be worth it, because once the surrounding thicket of foliage has been removed, these shrubs should grow neat and compact from then on. The gaps left where unsuitable plants have been taken out can be filled with compact shrubs and other small plants, and the garden will soon be looking good again.

USING TREES AND SHRUBS IN SMALL GARDENS

As mentioned previously, the role of trees and shrubs in a small garden is to provide shelter and privacy, as well as to act as a background to other smaller plants you may want to grow. There are several ways you can make room for shrubs, even in a small garden. But whichever you choose, don't pick only the smallest growing varieties – even a small garden needs a few taller or broader plants to give it shape and to create a screen for shelter from the prevailing wind, or to keep the garden from being overlooked.

As a general rule, try to avoid planting any tree within 10 ft (3 m) and preferably 15–20 ft (4.5–6 m), of the house, or where drains run under a garden. The latter is specially important for plants with water-seeking roots like Salix, Cornus, Hydrangea, as they can cause expensive blockages!

Garden Boundaries

Any garden needs something to mark its borders with those of its neighbours. In large gardens, formal hedges such as Beech, Hornbeam or a conifer like Leylands Cypress are often chosen, but in small gardens they are not suitable as they take up a lot of room. They also need a lot of clipping, besides making it difficult for anything much to grow alongside them, due to the very heavy shade they cast and their enormous uptake of water from the surrounding soil. This is why people often choose fencing such as interwoven or larch-lap types for small gardens. But while a fence certainly makes a convenient place to grow climbers and doesn't make the ground dry, it will nevertheless cast a lot of shade, and can cause more work than you might think by needing regular painting with wood preservative, not to mention attention after gales.

If you have no need for a high barrier round the edge of your garden, a low hedge of plants such as Lavender, Cistus or Hebe could fit the bill nicely. And being slightly less formal, it makes much less work – you only need to clip the plants roughly back into shape after flowering.

Or, if height is important, rather than having a solid hedge, you could plant an informal mixed border instead. By planting tall shrubs at the back, shorter shrubs in the middle and herbaceous and annual plants at the front, you could create the impression of a normal garden border, whilst at the same time producing an effective barrier. If a more impenetrable barrier is needed, the back row of shrubs could well include thorny types such as Berberis, Pyracantha, species Roses that would soon 'knit' together. Or choose evergreens which, even in a low hedge, give a feeling of solidness all year round.

LOW SHRUBS SUITABLE FOR HEDGING

BERBERIS THUNBERGII 'Atropurpurea Nana' – purple-leaved prickly plants said to repel dogs; to 2 ft (60 cm).

BERBERIS THUNBERGII 'Helmond Pillar' – striking, bolt upright growing plants, purple foliage; to 4 ft (120 cm).

BUXUS SEMPERVIRENS (Box) – makes a neat, low, evergreen hedge which can be kept as low as 6 ins (15 cm) or 1 ft (30 cm) by clipping.

CISTUS – evergreen plants smothered with large pink or mauve poppy-like flowers in summer; to 2 ft (60 cm). Good for very informal hedges.

HEBE – makes a pretty informal hedge that flowers all summer; to 2 ft 6 ins (75 cm).

LAVENDULA – an attractive semi-formal hedge with silvery-grey foliage and scented purple flowers on tall stems; to 2 ft (60 cm).

OLEARIA HAASTII – 'daisy bushes', with pretty silver triangular leaves and large fragrant daisy-like flowers in summer; to 4 ft (120 cm).

POTENTILLA – very sprawling, informal hedge with yellow flowers throughout summer; to 2 ft (60 cm).

PRUNUS CISTENA 'Crimson Dwarf' – semi-formal hedge with red leaves; to 3 ft (90 cm).

ROSEMARINUS OFFICINALIS 'Miss Jessups Upright' – slow-growing, upright variety which makes a neat, scented hedge; to 3–4 ft (90–120 cm) in time.

SANTOLINA (Cotton Lavender) – lacy, silvery foliage making a semi-formal hedge 2–3 ft (60–90 cm) high.

Evergreens and Conifers

Plants that retain their leaves in winter are the 'backbone' of a garden. And although with evergreens and conifers you do not enjoy the benefit of seasonal variation as you do with deciduous shrubs, they are particularly valuable in a small garden for their all-the-year-round effect. In planning a garden, these are the plants to position first. But apart from using them to establish the framework of the garden design, some kinds are also useful for their particular 'architectural' features. The striking shapes of some conifers, for instance, makes them specially suitable for creating eye-catching garden features. You can also use them to frame a particularly nice view to draw attention to it, or conversely, screen out an unpleasant one.

EVERGREENS

ARUNDINARIA VIRIDISTRIATA – golden yellow-striped leaves with faintly purple canes; 4 ft (120 cm).

BERBERIS BUXIFOLIA 'Nana' – neat dome-shaped prickly bushes, orange flowers in late spring and purple berries in autumn; to 2 ft (60 cm).

CHOISYA TERNATA (Mexican Orange Blossom) – scented foliage, and clusters of small white flowers in early summer; to 4 ft (120 cm).

CHOISYA TERNATA 'Sundance' – striking, golden-leaved form of above.

COTONEASTER SALICIFOLIUS FLOCCOSUS – long, narrow, shiny leaves, graceful arching stems and lots of small red berries in autumn; to 4 ft (120 cm).

ELAEAGNUS X EBBINGEI 'Limelight' – fast-growing, weather-tolerant shrub with densely packed oval-shaped leaves variegated in dark and lime green; to 6 ft (2 m).

ESCALLONIA – lots of small, shiny, deep-green leaves and plenty of smallish bell-shaped flowers in summer; some varieties tend to be tall and straggly – 'Peach Blossom' (orangey-pink flowers) and 'Apple Blossom' (pale pink flowers) both fairly compact and floriferous; to 4 ft (120 cm).

EUCALYPTUS – fast-growing trees with attractively peeling bark; plants can also be cut back hard and will then grow as shrubs. Most varieties withstand hard annual pruning to maintain a height of about 4–6 ft (1.2–1.8 m).

GARRYA ELLIPTICA – very slow-growing bushy tree with tough deep-green shiny leaves; covered with long green catkins in late winter and early spring; good for flower arrangers; to 8 ft (2.4 m) eventually.

MAHONIA JAPONICA and 'Charity' – both have large pinnate leaves, with individual leaflets rather like holly and equally prickly. Long racemes of yellow lily-of-the-valley scented flowers cascade from the tips of the stems in early spring, framed by a collar of foliage. Both grow to 5 ft (1.5 m).

MYRTUS (Myrtle) – rather tender aromatic plant; the common variety is COMMUNIS (3 ft/90 cm) with white flowers in midsummer followed by black berries, but TARANTINA is more free-flowering and has white berries; to 2 ft (60 cm).

OLEARIA MACRODONTA (New Zealand Holly) – a wind-tolerant 'daisy bush' with large, leathery, serrated leaves grey-green above and silvery beneath, and large white daisies.

PHORMIUM – clusters of long, narrow, spike-shaped leaves growing from a central crown – different varieties available with red, cream and green variegated or purplish foliage. Mature plants produce strange flowers; slightly tender in northern districts; to 4 ft (120 cm).

PHOTINIA FRASERI 'Red Robin' – slightly resembles Pieris but will grow on most soils. Deep green leaves, the tips of the new growth are brilliant red; white bell-shaped flowers appear in early summer; to 5 ft (1.5 m).

PIERIS 'Forest Flame' – young growth is flame red in spring, appears shortly after clusters of small white bell-like flowers. Height to 5 ft (1.5 m). *P. japonica* 'Variegata' has attractive cream/green variegated leaves; height 3 ft (90 cm). Needs acid soil.

RHODODENDRON – dwarf varieties such as 'Blue Diamond', 'Elizabeth', yakushimanum hybrids approximately 18 ins–2 ft (45–60 cm) high, slow growing, neat compact shapes.

ROSEMARINUS OFFICINALIS 'Miss Jessups Upright' – narrow upright shape to 3–4 ft (90–120 cm); 'McConnells Blue' is compact, hillock-shaped, 18 ins (45 cm) high, 3ft (90 cm) diameter.

RUTA GRAVEOLENS – low-growing, rounded-shaped aromatic shrub with glaucous blue foliage; to 2 ft (90 cm).

STRANSVAESIA DAVIDIANA 'Palette' – sensational colouration is most pronounced on young shoots which open red and soon develop pink, green and cream variegation; white flowers in mid summer and red berries in autumn; height 5–6 ft (1.5–1.8 m).

YUCCA FILAMENTOSA – arresting sight; spikey leaved sub-tropical-looking plants, 18 ins (45 cm) high, which flower with a cascade of giant creamy white bells suspended over the plant on a tall stem; to 4 ft (120 cm).

Mixed Borders

Having established the basic shape of the garden with ever-greens, small shrubs can be used to 'fill in' the details. Contrary to popular belief, shrubs do not have to be large bushy plants like the popular favourites you see everywhere – plenty of the more unusual or choice kinds are quite compact, ideal for small gardens. So, if you like interesting plants or just want something different, you can have them, because a small garden makes it possible to grow plants that need special care, or those which would easily get 'lost' amongst large shrubs in a big garden – or which cost just that little bit extra to buy. And now that small garden owners are creating a demand for unusual plants, plenty of small specialist nurseries are springing up to supply them. The net result is that you can have precisely the sort of garden you fancy. You could, for instance, opt for a Mediterranean-look garden, planted with shrubby herbs and grey-foliaged plants – all will look good together and grow well in a sunny southern garden with dryish soil. Or you could go for an old-fashioned cottage garden look, which is fast becoming popular once more. You could go for a garden based entirely on dwarf conifers, grasses and evergreens that would look good all year round yet need very little maintenance. And for a more traditional look but in miniature, you could choose compact varieties of 'old favourite' shrubs, with some of the smaller growing roses including the new ground-cover varieties and miniatures.

Island Beds

As a complete contrast to 'normal' borders which are generally arranged round the edge of a garden, with island beds it's the other way round – the beds are in the middle of the garden, with the lawn round the edge. Island beds are a relatively new idea, and one that is particularly suited to small gardens. They have nothing in common with the very formal rectangular or round beds you used to see cut into the middle of a front garden lawn. Modern island beds are very informal in shape – teardrop shaped being the most popular. The bed can be tailored to fit into the contours of the lawn on a sloping or uneven site, to make it look more interesting. But even in a level garden, island beds look good. You can have just one – or a group of several, placed together to create a much more interesting, almost patchwork-like, effect than you could get with a regular border.

Island beds are intended to be seen from all round, not just from the front like a 'normal' border, so when planning and planting them, put the tallest or evergreen plants to the centre, with smaller plants graduating down to the edges. Because you can get at them from all round, island beds are very much easier to weed than 'normal' beds too. They always look very striking, set off against the surrounding sea of lawn; and though they were originally used very successfully for combinations of conifers, heathers and grasses, they also look very good planted with a typical mixed border selection of plants. But they are the perfect way of showing off any group of plants that has been chosen to associate particularly well together.

PLANT ASSOCIATIONS BASED ON TREES AND SHRUBS
Conifers, heathers, bulbs, grasses.
Rhododendrons, Pieris, Birches, Epimedium.
Azaleas, *Acer palmatum dissectum*, Bamboos.

Corylus contorta, Bamboo, *Parrotia persica*.
Cornus alba, *Choisya ternata*, Helleborus.
Berberis 'Helmond Pillar', *Choisya ternata* 'Sundance', low ground-cover plants.

Climbers

You can use climbers or trained shrubs to cover a solid fence or wall, which makes it much more interesting to look at. A wall or fence also provides a nice sheltered environment in which to grow slightly tender plants that would probably not survive in the open garden. If you don't have a solid fence or wall, climbers can be planted to cover a chain-link fence which, in time, creates the effect of a narrow hedge. They can also be trained up through trees or shrubs with an otherwise short season to make them more interesting; the climber's flowers appear all over the tree or shrub it is climbing up, looking just like an extra crop of flowers. And they are useful for covering an old tree stump or outbuilding, turning what could easily be an eyesore into an attractive feature. Some climbers are distinctly over-vigorous for a small garden, so it is advisable to stick to less rampant kinds.

ABELIA – wall shrub; small shrubs with red or pink bell-shaped flowers from mid to late summer; to 4 ft (120 cm).

AKEBIA QUINATA – unusual climber with semi-evergreen leaves, purplish flowers and strange sausage-like purple fruits produced after a good summer. Good for covering old stumps or up through trees, etc.

AMPELOPSIS BREVIPEDUNCULATA 'Variegata' – another unusual climber, this time with very striking three-coloured variegated foliage in pink, cream and green; stems often die back to base after a cold winter.

ARISTOLOCHIA MACROPHYLLA (Dutchman's Pipe) – fairly vigorous climber with big heart-shaped leaves and extraordinary flowers rather like an Arum Lily but in greenish yellow with brownish purple markings. Definitely a conversation piece.

CHAENOMELES – any of the normal garden varieties can be trained onto a wall where they look most attractive.

CLEMATIS, HYBRIDS AND SPECIES – climbers ideal for rambling over old tree stumps, or through trees or shrubs.

CLIANTHUS PUNICEUS (Lobster Claw) – semi-evergreen climber with large and very spectacular flowers like bunches of bright red claws in early summer, ferny foliage. Slightly tender.

FREMONTADENDRON CALIFORNICA – wall shrub with large single yellow flowers, rather waxy in texture, and triangular evergreen leaves – needs a sheltered spot, slightly tender.

HEDERA HELIX 'Buttercup' (golden yellow) – Gold Heart (green with gold splash in centre of leaves), self-clinging climbers.

HUMULUS LUPULUS 'Aureus' (Golden Hop) – fast-growing climber with large, bright gold typically hop-like leaves, good for covering pergolas, outbuildings, etc. quickly without being over-invasive; tolerates cutting back to keep within bounds.

HYDRANGEA PETIOLARIS – very hardy climber which is self-clinging, large flat-faced typically Hydrangea-like flowers mid summer. Ideal for covering outbuildings, tree stumps, walls, etc.

LONICERA BROWNII 'Dropmore Scarlet' – climber with long slender tubular scarlet flowers produced mid to late summer.

PARTHENOCISSUS HENRYANA – much less vigorous climber than its cousin Virginia Creeper; henryana has prettily marked green, bronze and cream leaves.

PASSIFLORA (Passionflower) – slightly tender climber for a south wall, large showy blue/mauve flowers throughout summer, occasionally followed by edible fruit after warm weather.

ROSES (climbing varieties) – smaller climbers such as Cupid (single peach flowers), Danse du Feu (double scarlet), Ena Harkness (double crimson), Golden Showers (double gold, scented), Shot Silk (double salmon, scented), Zephirine Drouhin (double pink, scented and nearly thornless).

SOLANUM CRISPUM 'Glasnevin' – in time makes quite a large plant unless pruned, but a most spectacular and unusual climber with flowers similar to those of potato in blue and yellow.

VITUS VINIFERA 'Purpurea' – like a purple-leaved grapevine bearing small edible purple grapes after a warm summer; good for a sunny spot.

Ground-cover Plants

In large gardens, ground-cover plants are very often used as a means of cutting down on weeding. The idea is, that by covering all the soil beneath larger trees and shrubs with low-growing or creeping varieties, you can 'smother out' weed seedlings. In a small garden, the same technique can be used very satisfactorily to reduce routine chores. But what is even more useful where space is at a premium, is the extra layer of plants – and consequently greater interest – you can add to the garden by using the space underneath larger plants. You can use ground-cover plants in mixed borders, in island beds, with conifers, evergreen and deciduous shrubs, and as a backdrop for specimen plants or shrubs in containers. You can find evergreen ground-cover plants like Ivies, and *Euonymus fortunei* varieties such as 'Emerald n' Gold'; ground-coverers with berries in autumn, like *Gaultheria procumbens* or some of the prostrate Cotoneasters, or flowering ground-cover like Heathers. But as always, the trick is to choose ground-cover plants that complement the shrubs they are growing between, for the most attractive effect.

GOOD GROUND-COVER PLANTS FOR SMALL GARDENS

COTONEASTER ADPRESSUS, DAMMERI, HORIZONTALIS, SALICIFOLIUS 'Repens' – all ground-hugging and spreading with red berries in autumn. *Adpressus* has good autumn tints to its leaves, the rest are all evergreen.

ERICA, CALLUNA (Heathers) – make dense carpets up to a foot thick in time; clip over with shears after flowering to keep tidy.,

EPIMEDIUM – fascinating, low-sprawling shrubs with heart-shaped leaves marked with red; *rubrum* is the brightest coloured. Small yellow or red flowers in spring. Height around 1 ft (30 cm).

EUONYMUS FORTUNEI – low evergreen variegated shrubs, deep-green shiny leaves variegated with silver or gold, stems 1–2 ft (30–60 cm) high.

GAULTHERIA PROCUMBENS – evergreen carpeter producing white flowers in spring and a profusion of large red berries in autumn; 1 ft (30 cm) maximum.

JUNIPERUS – low spreading varieties especially *J. horizontalis* varieties ('Turquoise Spreader', turquoise; 'Grey Pearl', grey;

67

'Blue Chip', silvery blue; or 'Prince of Wales', bright green in summer, bronzey purple in winter). *J. media* varieties ('Gold Coast', bright golden; 'Mint Julep', bright green; 'Sulphur Spray', bright yellow with whitish highlights). Height eventually to 3 ft (90 cm), spreads to 6 ft (1.8 m).

LEUCOTHOE FONTANESIANA 'Rainbow' – brilliantly coloured graceful shrubs that tolerate quite heavy shade; leaves variegated with pink, cream, green and yellow. White flowers produced in early summer the full length of the stems. To 2 ft (60 cm).

PACHYSANDRA TERMINALIS 'Variegata' – eyecatching carpet of short-stemmed green and cream variegated plants with leaves balanced on tops of stems like small parasols; spreads slowly, height 4–6 ins (10–15 cm).

POTENTILLA – slightly sprawling plants that can become untidy unless clipped back into shape after flowering. Smothered in red, orange or yellow Cinquefoil-like flowers in summer. Height to 2 ft (60 cm).

ROSE 'Nozomi' – ground-cover roses are one of the newer ideas, and look very nice if you don't mind weeding between prickly ground-cover plants. 'Nozomi' is particularly pretty, covering the ground in single pink flowers, a bit like more sophisticated versions of the wild Dog Rose. Plant spreads slowly, and is completely prostrate.

VINCA (Periwinkle) – common plants but the double form is very pretty and more unusual. Ideal for heavily shaded or woodland gardens where nothing much else grows at ground level and you want a 'natural' look.

Specimen Plants

The idea of having a single, large specimen tree such as a Weeping Willow in the middle of the front lawn has, fortunately, now gone out of fashion. Weeping Willows were far too big for the small gardens they were usually planted in and soon swamped everything in sight – often including the house. Nowadays a less formal style of gardening is in vogue, and front gardens are usually planted much more interestingly. Today, a specimen plant is more likely to be planted as a backdrop to an island bed, tucked into a corner, or even planted in a pot on a patio. An idea that is becoming increasingly popular is the planting of a tight group of small specimen plants, to create an even more back-to-nature look – three Birches for instance make a much more interesting shape than a single one (use the normal Birch, *Betula pendula*, or one of the 'fancy' kinds). Or you can plant a small 'specimen group' into the lawn – perhaps a Birch with a miniature Rhododendron underneath. This makes it very easy to use specimen plants in back gardens too.

What makes a good specimen plant? Basically it can be any variety that looks good standing on its own. The most successful examples are plants with a strongly defined shape, or some particularly striking feature that makes them stand out. Some good examples are given below.

GOOD SPECIMEN PLANTS

ACER PALMATUM varieties – 'Atropurpureum' has brilliant reddish-purple palmate leaves; 'Dissectum' has finely divided bright-green leaves looking like lace; 'Dissectum Atropurpureum' is similar but with reddish-purple leaves.

ARUNDINARIA NITIDA – tall, typically bamboo-like canes but very slender and black in colour. Spreads slowly by underground rhizomes.

BETULA (Birch) – graceful small trees that cast very light shade allowing other plants to be grown beneath their canopy; *Pendula youngii*, a small weeping tree, golden autumn foliage, to 8 ft (2.4 m); *Betula pendula* 'Purpurea', unusual birch with purple leaves and stems, to 20 ft (6 m), in time; *Betula pendula* 'Fastigiata', very straight upright grower, to 15 ft (4.5 m) eventually.

CORNUS ALTERNIFOLIA 'Argentea' – a member of the Dogwood family but totally unlike its better-known relatives; forms a most spectacular small bushy tree with branches arranged in tiers, leaves are cream and green variegated. Needs a sheltered spot; slow growing; height to 6–7 ft (1.8–2.1 m).

EUCALYPTUS – an ideal subject for planting in groups of three, or a single plant cut back to produce several stems. *Nifofila* (Snow Gum) is one of the hardiest, and very attractive with grey/beige patterned trunks of peeling bark, drooping habit and long grey-green leaves. Cut back whenever necessary (in spring) to keep at a suitable height.

MORUS ALBA 'Pendula' (Weeping Mulberry) – beautiful small tree producing a tumbling cascade of branches down to ground level;

to 7 ft (2.1m). Its cousin the White Mulberry has large heart-shaped leaves and edible fruit, though this is not the true fruiting Mulberry; 8 ft (2.4 m).

RHUS TYPHINA 'Laciniata' – a less common form of the Sumach, *Rhus typhina*; this one has very finely divided leaves and brilliant flame red and orange autumn colouring. Makes a lovely small tree; to 7 ft (2.1 m).

SOPHORA JAPONICA (Japanese Pagoda Tree) – small tree with a distinctive rounded shape and an oriental air about it, with large compound leaves made up of many individual leaflets. Cream flowers, resembling those of peas, produced in summer; height to 6 ft (1.8 m).

Trees and Shrubs in Pots

As gardens have become smaller, and more and more people have patios, it is now becoming very fashionable to garden in pots and other sorts of containers. Apart from the decorative aspects, there are two very good reasons for doing so – for one thing, there is virtually no work to do apart from watering and feeding, and for another, by restricting plants in pots they stay quite a bit smaller than they would do in a border. Virtually any of the smaller shrubs and dwarf or slow-growing conifers are suitable for growing in pots; you need 15–18 in. (37.5–45 cm) pots and either John Innes potting compost, or an ericaceous compost for lime-haters like Rhododendrons. You can use a single 'architecturally shaped' shrub as a specimen, such as Fatsia, *Acer palmatum* 'Dissectum', the contorted hazel *Corylus contorta*, or maybe a miniature conifer; alternatively you could make a group of individually potted shrubs, either as a display on their own or to use as a background to summer-flowering annuals.

However you choose to arrange them, shrubs grown in pots all year round need the same sort of winter care as pot-grown fruit trees. Protect the roots from severe frost by either lagging the pots with newspaper, sinking them into the ground, or put them in a cold greenhouse during the worst of the weather. Tender varieties such as Myrtle etc. can be stood inside a cold or frost-free greenhouse for winter protection. And remember to keep all potted shrubs very well fed and watered in summer – check them at least once a day to see if they need watering, and add a dose of liquid feed to their water once a week.

SPECIALLY GOOD TREES AND SHRUBS FOR CONTAINERS

ARUNDINARIA (Bamboo) – striking plants for containers; keep well watered in summer but not waterlogged.

BERBERIS – any of the very compact varieties such as *buxifolius* 'Nana', 'Corallina Compacta'.

BUXUS SEMPERVIRENS – very slow-growing, compact bushes; can be trained into fashionable minature topiary shapes; ideal for garden urns etc.

CAMELLIA – plant in ericaceous compost, and keep in a cold greenhouse in winter – in cold areas you can keep it under cold glass until after it has flowered to protect blooms from damage.

DAPHNE – *cneorum* has delightfully scented flowers produced in early spring on bare stems, 1 ft (30 cm); *mezereum* is better known, very early spring flowers are purple, height to 2 ft (60 cm).

FATSIA JAPONICA – striking 'architectural' evergreen plant with large palmate (hand-shaped) leaves, unusual white flowers in late summer/autumn.

HEBE – excellent potted shrub; the variegated *Hebe x andersonii* 'Variegata' is tender and needs protection in winter.

MYRTUS (Myrtle) – aromatic evergreen plant with white flowers in summer; *communis* has black berries in autumn, height 3 ft (90 cm); *tarantina* is freer flowering and has white berries, 2 ft (60 cm).

PHORMIUM – a very striking patio plant, many need winter protection in cold area.

PIERIS – plant in ericaceous compost; makes a good potted specimen plant.

RHODODENDRON (dwarf varieties) – grow in ericaceous compost.

SALVIA (Ornamental Sage) – Red Sage (with purple leaves) and Tricolor Sage are both most attractive and team up well with annual bedding plants.

YUCCA – adds a Mediterranean touch to a patio with its spikey rosette of leaves and tall cascading shower of white flowers; to 4 ft (120 cm) when flowering.

CONIFERS FOR CONTAINERS

CHAMAECYPARIS LAWSONIANA 'Ellwoods Pillar' – a miniature version of the classic narrow, upright spire-shaped conifer; feathery blue-grey foliage; height to 3 ft (90 cm).

CHAMAECYPARIS OBTUSA 'Nana Gracilis' – a real miniature, with crisp, curly, deep-green foliage; slow-growing; height 1 ft (30 cm).

CHAMAECYPARIS OBTUSA 'Tetragona Aurea' – most unusual shape like an irregularly twisted spire in green and gold; mossy foliage; very distinctive; height 3 ft (90 cm).

CHAMAECYPARIS PISIFERA 'Boulevard' – very popular blue pyramidal conifer; to 4 ft (120 cm).

CHAMAECYPARIS PISIFERA 'Filifera Aurea' – very unusual foliage like heaps of bright yellow string; mound-shaped plants a bit like haystacks from a distance; height 2–3 ft (60–90 cm).

CRYPTOMERIA JAPONICA 'Vilmoriniana' – ultra compact foliage grows into an uneven mound shape suggesting it has been sculpted by the wind; very slow growing; height 1 ft (30 cm).

JUNIPERUS SQUAMATA 'Blue Star' – broad, bushy conifer, one of the best blues available; height to 18 ins (45 cm).

PICEA PUNGENS ALBERTIANA 'Conica' – perfectly pyramidal, with neat clusters of short needles forming the shape; slow growing; height to 4 ft (120 cm).

Trees and Shrubs for Problem Places

Large gardens often offer a choice of soil types and situations, so it is usually possible to find somewhere suitable for just about anything you may want to grow. In small gardens this is less likely to be the case. And while you can improve less-than-perfect conditions in some cases, it is more common to find you need to choose plants that enjoy or at least tolerate what you have got. Here are some of the commonest 'problem areas', and trees and shrubs you can grow in them. (NB: Plenty of tolerant plants will put up with more than one set of adverse conditions!)

DRY SUN

ABELIA	LAVENDULA	SALVIA
BERBERIS	OLEARIA	SANTOLINA

TOP Up the wall – vertical gardening makes use of every scrap of
space. Here a shed wall has been covered in rustic trellis and used
to hang wall baskets. Butchers' hooks have been used for hanging
the basket; they are very convenient and easily taken down if need
be.

BOTTOM A stone sink planted with alpines makes an attractive
compact garden feature. The container echoes the natural habitat
of the plants.

ABOVE Wild corner planted with ox-eye daisies – the wild theme teams up well with the hurdle fence and unusual rustic path.

(OPPOSITE PAGE)
TOP Using a strimmer to tidy long grass at the edge of a wall.
BOTTOM Electric lawn edger at work neatening edges after mowing.

ABOVE Seed sower, which automatically spaces out seeds, avoiding
bending when you sow, or thinning out later.

(OPPOSITE PAGE)
TOP Electric lawn raker removes moss and 'thatch' from lawns the
easy way. It can also be used to sweep leaves from the lawn in autumn.
BOTTOM Manual (push) lawn edge trimmer.

Gravel makes an unusual and attractive permanent mulch, which is specially good for plants that like good drainage.

Border mulched with a deep layer of flint chippings – an ornamental and permanent mulch.

An easy alternative to tying plants up to canes for support – here the shoots grow up through the 'grid', which holds them unobtrusively as it is hidden by foliage most of the time. It is also a lot less work than tying plants up to canes, you just site it in place when growth starts in spring and remove it when clearing old foliage from the bed in autumn.

BUXUS	PHLOMIS FRUCTICOSA	SENECIO LAXIFOLIUS
CERATOSTIGMA WILLMOTTIANUM	PHORMIUM	SPIRAEA
CISTUS	POTENTILLA	TAMARIX
GENISTA	RHUS	ULEX
HEBE	RIBES	YUCCA
HIBISCUS	ROMNEYA COULTERI	
HYPERICUM	ROSEMARINUS	

DAMP SHADE

ACER PALMATUM VARIETIES	GAULTHERIA PROCUMBENS	RHODODENDRON (DWARF VARIETIES)
CAMELLIA	HEDERA	RUSCUS
CORNUS	PACHYSANDRA	VINCA
DANAE RACEMOSA	PERNETTYA	
DECAISNEA FARGESII	PIERIS	

DRY SHADE (under trees etc.)

BERBERIS	ILEX	SALVIA
BUXUS	PACHYSANDRA	SANTOLINA
DANAE RACEMOSA	RHUS	SKIMMIA
HEDERA	RIBES	

MOIST SOIL IN SUN OR PARTIAL SUN

AMELANCHIER	CORYLUS CONTORTA	PERNETTYA
BETULA PENDULA	LABURNUM	SALIX
CORNUS	PAROTTIA PERSICA	SPIRAEA

ACID SOIL

ERICA, CALLUNA (Heathers)	KALMIA	RHODODENDRON
FOTHERGILLA	LEUCOTHOE	
GAULTHERIA	PERNETTYA	

Other Useful/Interesting Trees and Shrubs for Small Gardens

AMELANCHIER LAMARCKII – young foliage copper coloured, masses of white flowers in April; autumn tints and berries; height 9 ft (2.7 m).

ARBUTUS UNEDO – small bushy evergreen tree with pinkish-white bell-like flowers in spring, followed by large round red rough-skinned fruits which persist well into winter; eventual height about 8–10 ft (2.4–3 m).

ARTEMESIA – sub-shrubs with bright silver leaves that make good 'foils' for colourful flowering plants such as Cistus, Dianthus or annual bedding plants; suit dry sunny spot best; foliage is aromatic in some varieties – 'Powis Castle' forms a mound shape 2 ft (60 cm) high; *absinthium* 'Lambrook Silver' is shrubbier with frothy yellow flowers, 18 ins (45 cm).

CORNUS ALBA 'Elegantissima' (silver variegated leaves) and 'Spaethii' (gold variegated leaves) – both have striking red stems which are most noticeable in winter when the leaves have fallen from them. These contrast well with green or blue evergreens. To 4 ft (120 cm).

CORYLUS CONTORTA (Corkscrew Hazel, Harry Lauder's Walking Stick) – slow-growing bushy tree with strangely twisted stems which are most noticeable in winter when the leaves have fallen from them; also produces (normal) yellow catkins in spring – useful for flower arrangers. Eventually reaches about 10 ft (3 m).

CYTISUS KEWENSIS – small broom with dense evergreen leaves covered with creamy yellow pea-like flowers in spring; slightly weeping, makes it good for growing at the edge of steps, or at the edge of a wall where it can trail a little; 18 ins (45 cm).

DECAISNEA FARGESII (Bean Tree) – unusual tall shrubby plant to about 10 ft (3 m); not specially remarkable greenish flowers in spring followed in autumn by extraordinary big blue pods like huge metallic runner beans. Large leaves.

FUCHSIA – hardy varieties are very useful for summer colour; flowers produced freely all summer. Branches die back to ground level in winter, protect crowns with ashes in cold areas. Height 3–4 ft (90–120 cm).

HIBISCUS – hardy Hibiscus are as exotic as the indoor varieties but much tougher, *H. syriacus* 'Blue Bird' has large single blue flowers, *syriacus* 'Hamabo' has large single pale pink flowers with red centres, 'Jean d'arc' has semi-double white flowers. Height 4–6 ft (1.2–1.8 m), grow in sheltered sunny spot.

NANDINIA PYGMAEA 'Fire Power' (Sacred Bamboo) – not a Bamboo at all, but a low-growing shrub with rather tall upright stems and large leaves that have very spectacular autumn colouring. These are often retained throughout winter for a useful show of colour when there is not much around. Clusters of white flowers throughout summer; red berries in autumn. Height 3–4 ft (90–120 cm).

PARROTIA PERSICA – flowers in March producing a mass of brilliant crimson stamens; good autumn colour. Older trees have attractively peeling bark.

PEROVSKIA 'Blue Spire' – aromatic sub-shrub with grey foliage contrasting nicely with large sprays of tightly packed lavender blue flowers from mid summer to early autumn. Height 2 ft (60 cm).

PRUNUS AMANOGAWA – compact, upright growing Flowering Cherry, smothered in pink flowers April/May; height 6–8 ft (1.8–2.4 m).

SAMBUCUS RACEMOSA 'Plumosa Aurea' – very striking golden form of Elder with attractively cut leaves and red berries in autumn. Slow growing and beautifully coloured; 5–6 ft (1.5–1.8 m).

WEIGELA FLORIDA 'foliis purpurea' – a 'different' version of an old favourite, with dark pink flowers contrasting vividly with purple foliage – 3 ft (90 cm); also interesting is *florida* 'Variegata' which has green/cream variegated leaves and pale pink flowers – 4 ft (120 cm).

ROUTINE CARE OF TREES AND SHRUBS

In a large garden, you could get by with just planting shrubs, doing virtually nothing more to them apart from occasionally feeding, or perhaps removing the odd dead branch. But in a small garden, each plant really counts and has to earn its keep by constantly looking its best – right from the moment it is planted. So it is worthwhile spending a bit of time just when it's needed, taking the right sort of care of them.

Getting New Plants Established

Getting new trees and shrubs off to a flying start depends on planting them properly in the first place. And unless your soil is naturally very good indeed, it is well worth digging in as much

well-rotted organic material or peat as you can; not just to the
bottom of the hole where the shrub is to be planted, but to the
whole of the bed. It really is quite amazing the difference this
apparently simple job makes to the speed with which plants get
established, and to the time they take to fill the space allocated to
them. You can have a mature-looking border in a couple of years,
which otherwise may have taken ten or fifteen years to achieve.
During the time new plants are finding their feet, it is essential to
keep them well watered whenever the soil starts to get dry –
certainly in summer, but possibly at other times of year too,
depending on the weather. Once shrubs are starting to grow, they
can be reckoned to be starting to get established and from then on
it is a good idea to begin feeding them. Feed with any general-
purpose feed – Growmore can be sprinkled on the ground at 2–4
oz (55–110 g) per square yard (metre) when growth starts in
spring and again about eight weeks later (water well afterwards
if the ground is dry), or you can water on diluted liquid or soluble
feed once every few weeks during the growing season – whichever
is the more convenient.

Pruning

For the little time it takes, it is worth doing the odd bit of pruning
when it is needed, to keep plants in check, in shape and constantly
productive in whatever you planted them for – flowers, foliage,
berries or what-have-you. In general, shrubs don't need any
regular pruning – 'when it is needed' is the operative phrase.

'When it is needed' may be when you first plant a new tree or
shrub. Perhaps the plant is not a very good shape, having, say, a
couple of long thin stems when it should be nice and bushy. In this
case, cut it back to about 4–6 ins (10–15 cm) above the top of the
pot, and it will soon start to branch out again from nearer the
base. If the plant is cluttered with lots of little twiggy bits, these
can be cut right back to the main stems to leave a clean bushy
shape.

After planting, when plants have had a few years to grow, it is
likely they will occasionally need tidying up; perhaps after a
severe winter or storm has made the ends of the shoots die back or
broken some entirely. These can be cut back to the next outward-
facing bud below the lowest part of the damage. And if, by the
time shrubs are very well established and large and they start to
grow straggly, or untidy, a little extra pruning may be called for.

In the case of flowering shrubs, you can prune out the entire stems responsible, either back to a natural junction with another better placed shoot, or right back to the base of the plant. At the same time you can thin out the weakest shoots in the same way, if the shrub is overcrowded with shoots. The best time for doing this is immediately after flowering, for late winter- and spring-flowering shrubs, and between leaf fall in autumn and bud burst in spring for summer- or autumn-flowering types.

With plants grown for foliage or colour the same general rule applies, but in certain cases it pays to be more drastic. Where the shrub is a vigorous one, and it is the juvenile leaves that produce the best coloration such as *Weigela* 'Flame', or with shrubs grown for colourful winter stems such as Cornus and *Salix viticella*, all of the oldest shoots should be cut right back to the base of the plants in late March. (You can easily tell which are the oldest stems as they turn a brownish colour, while the young stems retain their bright yellow, or red coloration.) Eucalyptus can be cut and treated even more severely; to make them continue producing the more interesting shaped juvenile foliage (which is often circular as against the long narrow adult foliage), cut them back almost to ground level every few years – it has the same effect as a bush fire back home in Australia, and most varieties will usually regenerate rapidly.

Shrubs grown for fruit or berries can't be pruned much without wrecking a year's fruiting. If you prune after flowering, you certainly won't get any berries that year; if you prune in early spring after the berries are finished you may find, with shrubs that flower on the current year's shoots, that they don't have time to grow the new growth to flower on. So as a general rule, try not to prune this group any more than is absolutely necessary to remove dead or diseased bits, and keep them tidy – and then take out whole branches or prune to a shoot junction, rather than snipping lots of little bits off here and there.

Chapter 4

Flowers

In a small garden, herbaceous and annual flowers are invaluable for adding colour. They create an ever-changing sequence of patterns, textures and hues that alters almost daily as different plants come in and out of flower. Set against a backdrop of trees, shrubs and evergreens in a mixed border, flowers are seen at their best; they are also the perfect way of adding seasonal highlights to an otherwise 'low-labour' garden, or making an instant display on a patio.

Over the past few years a few subtle changes have taken place, not only to the varieties of flowers we grow, but also to the way we grow them. Now, new varieties and growing methods together with changing gardening have made flower growing easier, more rewarding, and more foolproof than it has ever been before. But in a small garden, flowers have to work hard to justify the space they occupy. Varieties with long flowering seasons, compact habits, and low upkeep are now firm favourites. What is also a good idea where space is short, is to choose flowers that have more to offer than just looking pretty in the garden – varieties which are also good for cutting or drying for winter decoration indoors; that provide scent; or attract wildlife into the garden.

Whatever sort of scheme you want, there are flowers to help you create it. In a small garden, they can be regarded as the 'last touches' to your exterior decoration!

PROPAGATING TECHNIQUES

Raising Bedding Plants from Seed – under Glass

When you buy bedding plants from a garden centre, there is a very good chance that the grower who grew them will have used a new, cheaper production technique – growing in 'cells'. This way, instead of sowing the seed and then pricking the seedlings out

78

into trays as usual, he will have sown individual seeds straight into tiny containers – cells – each of which is a small finger-shaped compartment in a much larger tray of similar cells. Each cell is tapered so when the tray is filled with compost, you get a 'plug' of compost which is just big enough for a single plant. Naturally this makes it much cheaper to grow bedding plants as it takes much less compost than the traditional method. It also saves time, as there is no pricking out to do.

But growing in cells is no longer a technique only for commercial growers – you can do the same thing at home. Several different sorts of divided trays are on sale in garden centres. The only difference is that whereas commercial growers use a machine to sow pelleted seeds (single seeds coated with clay to make them easier to handle) one per cell, at home you can't often obtain pelleted seed. In this case, either sow five or six ordinary seeds into each cell and pull out the weakest seedlings, or simply use the containers for pricking out into. Not only does growing in cells save compost, it also makes life very much easier at planting-out time. Instead of tearing the roots apart trying to pull a tangle of plants out of trays, each plant is a separate individual. To get the plants out of their cells, just take an old dinner fork, cut off the central prongs to leave only the outside two, and use this to skewer each plug of roots. Then simply lift it out, and pop it into the soil. Because they don't suffer any root disturbance, cell-raised plants grow away without a check – so they are quickly established and start flowering well.

There are, however, a couple of points to watch if you grow in cells. One is that the plants need feeding and watering much more frequently than they would in trays or normal-sized pots. This is because they are growing in such a small volume of compost that it quickly gets depleted of water and nutrients. The other is that it is essential to plant as soon as the cell fills with roots – otherwise they very soon spoil. This means calculating sowing dates very carefully so you don't have to 'hold' plants for long once they are ready to plant. As a rough guide, sow slow growers like *Begonia semperflorens* and Lobelia in early March, and faster annuals like Salvia, French Marigold, etc. in mid to late March in a propagator, grow them on in a slightly heated greenhouse in good light, and they should be ready to go out towards the end of May. If they don't look like being on schedule, you can always speed them up by turning up the heat a bit at night, or slow them down by standing them outdoors during the day. Either way, harden them off properly by moving them into a cold frame for a week or two before planting them out.

Raising Hardy Annual Bedding Plants from Seed – in the Open

If you don't have a heated greenhouse to raise seedlings in, or don't fancy the amount of work involved pricking out bedding plants, you can always sow hardy annuals such as Clarkia, Nigella, Sweet Peas, straight into the ground. Half hardies such as Salvia, Petunias, French Marigolds, are not suitable for growing this way as, being tender, you could not sow the seed till late May and the resulting plants would not start flowering till the end of the summer. However, hardy annuals can be sown safely outdoors as soon as the soil is in workable condition from mid March onwards. Either sow them in rows in a spare bit of ground (an empty bit of the vegetable garden is ideal) and transplant the seedlings when they are big enough, or scatter the seed on well-prepared soil where you want the plants to flower. Of the two, the second saves an awful lot of work. But it should only be attempted if your ground has been well cultivated for years and is relatively free of weeds – otherwise when seedlings come up you can't tell what is what, and hoeing becomes a nightmare. But in a clean bit of land, all you need do is fork the soil over, rake a dressing of peat and general-purpose fertiliser such as Growmore into the top 2 ins (50 mm), and mark out the areas where you want to sow the different varieties with the point of a cane.

The pattern that looks best, once the plants are up and flowering, is a fairly informal arrangement of irregularly shaped interlocking patches, with the taller varieties being sown in the patches at the back of the border and the shorter ones towards the front. After sowing, rake lightly over to cover the seed and water the bed well. Or, on soil that tends to form a crust when it dries out, instead of raking the seed in, use one of the techniques originally intended to assist germination of direct-sown vegetable crops, and sprinkle a fine layer of vermiculite or peat over the seed instead. This way, you should get a much better 'stand' of seedlings.

HARDY ANNUALS

ALYSSUM	GYPSOPHILA	NASTURTIUM
CALENDULA	LARKSPUR	NEMOPHILA

CANDYTUFT	LAVATERA	NIGELLA
CLARKIA	LEPTOSIPHON	POPPY
CONVOLVULUS	LIMNATHES	SUNFLOWER
CORNFLOWER	LINARIA	SWEET PEAS
CREPIS	LINUM	SWEET SULTAN
ECHIUM	LOVE-LIES-BLEEDING	TROPAEOLUM CANARIENSE
ESCHSCHOLZIA	MATTHIOLA	VISCARIA
GODETIA	MIGNONETTE	VIRGINIA STOCK

Sowing Hardy Annuals in Autumn

Yet another way of getting round the problem of propagating your own plants without too much in the way of sophisticated equipment, is to sow hardy annuals under cold glass in the autumn. This has been done for many years with Sweet Peas, but lots of other hardy annuals can be treated the same way too. And just like Sweet Peas, you can keep the plants under cold frames or in an unheated greenhouse or glass porch for the winter – and the resulting plants will give you a much earlier show of flowers the following year than those sown in spring. What's more, some of the dwarfer varieties make very showy pot plants, so you don't have to put them all out in the garden!

For autumn sowing, sow seeds in mid to late September, and prick the seedlings out into trays (give them extra generous spacing) or 3½ in (85 mm) pots as soon as they are big enough – they will remain in these throughout the winter. If you want extra special plants, and particularly if you want to use them as pot plants, pot up the best in March into 5 in (12.5 cm) pots. (Specially successful varieties as pot plants are Antirrhinum, Calendula, Clarkia, Godetia and Nasturtium.) The rest can be hardened off by standing them outdoors during the day for a few weeks, then planted outside in the garden from early April, depending on the weather.

Raising Herbaceous Plants from Seed – under Glass

You can raise herbaceous plants from seed very easily just by sowing them outside and transplanting the seedlings to a 'nursery bed' until they are big enough to plant in the garden. But there is often a lot of wastage this way, with many plants that do not make a good size and consequently do not flower well in their first year. It also takes up a lot of space, as you normally need to grow more plants than you need to allow for those that don't make the grade. A much better way, if space is short, is to raise the plants more intensively using a very similar method to that used for hardy annuals.

Sow herbaceous plant seed rather earlier than for annuals – in June or July. Sow in a shady cold frame, in trays or directly into the soil, or else straight into well-prepared ground such as a spare row in the vegetable garden. Prick the seedlings out into further trays, giving them fairly generous spacing. Or, if they are in the garden, thin the seedlings to about 4–6 ins (10–15 cm) apart. When they are big enough, around mid September, pot each plant individually. A 4–5 in (10–12.5 cm) pot is best, or alternatively use those black plastic pots that look like plastic bags. Then move the plants into a cold frame, porch or cold greenhouse for the winter, and they'll be just right for planting out in March or April. True, this method is a bit more trouble than the traditional way – but you will get uniformly sized, top-quality plants which will flower well right from their first year in the garden – and which take up much less room while you are producing them.

NEW VARIETIES OF FLOWERS – AND A NEW KIND OF FLOWER GARDENING

Herbaceous Plants

Not so long ago, herbaceous plants were only sold in winter as uninteresting-looking roots – it was impossible to tell whether they were alive or dead. Nowadays they can be bought growing in containers virtually all the year round, and planted at any time – even whilst actually in flower. So if your carefully planned tree and shrub scheme seems to call for a splash of colour to brighten up an odd corner, you don't have to wait for the 'right' time of year to add to it. Nor do you have to stick with a garden that looks exactly the same from one year to the next, because herbaceous plants are easily dug up and moved – spring or autumn are the best time for this. What's more, they are easily divided up to make a few original plants cover a much larger area. Herbaceous plants don't have to be a lot of work these days, either. The newer varieties have been specially bred to be dwarf, so that many kinds are now self-supporting and don't need to be staked – even things like Delphiniums. And if you grow them in island beds, you'll have less work still. The traditional herbaceous bed created endless weeding and pest and disease control because, being backed by a hedge, it was notoriously well supplied with such nuisances – not to mention being difficult to get at to tackle any of them. And modern island beds, being out in the open, provide a healthier environment for plants and are easier to get at when you do have to weed.

DWARF VARIETIES OF HERBACEOUS PLANTS
ARUNCUS PLUMOSUS 'Glasnevin' – Goat's Beard with creamy plumes of flower to 4 ft (1.2 m) instead of usual 5–6 ft (1.5–1.8 m).
ASTILBE – 'Bronze Excellence', 'Sprite', 'William Buchanan', all about 9–10 ins (22–25 cm).
BEARDED IRIS – 'Austrian Sky', 'Beechfield', 'Bright Eyes', 'Lemon Flare', 'Lillywhite', 'Pogo', 'Tinkerbelle'; all around 1 ft (30 cm).
DELPHINIUMS – 'Blue Fountains', 'Blue Heaven', 3 ft (90 cm).
HEREMOCALLIS – 'Stella D'Oro', 2 ft (60 cm).
KNIPHOFIA – 'Candlelight', 'Little Maid'; 2 ft (60 cm).
LUPINS – 'Dwarf Lulu', 2 ft (60 cm).
MICHAELMAS DAISY – 'Little Pink Beauty', 'Audrey', 'Jenny', 'Snowsprite', 'Kristina'; approximately 1 ft (30 cm) high.
PAPAVER ORIENTALIS (Oriental Poppy) – 'Ladybird', 2 ft (60 cm).
SOLIDAGO (Golden Rod) – 'Cloth of Gold', 'Crown of Rays', 18 ins (45 cm); 'Golden Thumb', 1 ft (30 cm).

Annuals

Annual bedding too has seen a great many changes over the last few years. Instead of the once-popular carpet-bedding schemes with plants laid out in straight rows, nowadays a more relaxed style of gardening is fashionable, and bedding plants are more often used in informal groups in mixed borders, or in patio tubs, hanging baskets and window boxes. If you want something colourful to fill a gap in a hurry, annuals are the plants to go for. You can plant them in flower, for a superb display straight away. Annuals also make it possible for you to change the 'mood' of your garden every year without major upheavals, just by putting in different types of plant. You could choose a different colour scheme or style every time you re-plant – perhaps create a cottage-garden look, a semi-tropical look, a scented garden, or a more formal garden – all with a few bedding plants. Yet they are inexpensive to buy and easy to look after. And again, many of the newer varieties have been specially bred with dwarf habits to suit smaller gardens and particularly patio containers, for which they are ideally suited. The very dwarf varieties also make good pot plants for a greenhouse, conservatory, porch or even a sunny windowsill indoors. One big advantage of naturally compact varieties is that they need much less work than usual – no pinching out growing tips to make them bushy, or staking to keep them upright.

DWARF VARIETIES OF POPULAR ANNUALS

AFRICAN MARIGOLDS – 'Inca hybrids', 12 ins (30 cm).

ANTIRRHINUM – 'Magic Carpet'; 'Tom Thumb', 6 ins (15 cm); 'New Dwarf', 9 ins (22.5 cm).

ASTER – 'Contraster', 'Pot n' Patio', 'Thousand Wonders', 'Pinocchio', 'Blue Skies'; all around 6–8 ins (15–20 cm).

CALENDULA – 'Fiesta Gitana', 12 ins (30 cm).

COSMOS – 'Sunny Gold'; 'Sunny Red', 12–15 ins (30–37.5 cm).

DAHLIAS (bedding varieties) – 'Dwarf Anmore', 12 ins (30 cm); 'Bambino', 'Figaro', 'Rigoletto', 15 ins (37.5 cm).

DIGITALIS (Foxglove) – 'Foxy', 3 ft (90 cm).

HIBISCUS (bedding) – 'Disco Belle', 18 ins (45 cm).

HOLLYHOCK – 'Majorette', 2 ft 6 ins (75 cm); 'Pinafore', 3 ft 6 ins (105 cm).

IMPATIENS (Busy Lizzie) – 'Florette', 8 ins (20 cm).

NASTURTIUM – *nanum* varieties such as 'Alaska', 'Whirlybird', 'Empress of India'; all non-trailing, compact plants about 9 ins (22 cm).

NICOTIANA – 'Domino', 'Breakthrough', 'Nicki'; 12 ins (30 cm).

OSTEOSPERMUM – 'Dwarf Salmon', 9 ins (22 cm).

SWEET PEAS – 'bush' types suitable for hanging baskets, are self-supporting grown in groups in borders or as low annual hedges: 'Jet Set', 3 ft (90 cm); 'Bijou', 12 ins (30 cm); 'Cupid', 4 ins (10 cm).

SWEET WILLIAM – 'Indian Carpet', 6 ins (15 cm).

WALLFLOWER – 'Tom Thumb Mixed', 9 ins (22 cm).

Bulbs

The way we use bulbs has changed a lot in recent years, too. When very formal gardens were the fashion, bulbs used to be treated rather like bedding plants, set out in straight rows in special beds of their own, and dug up after flowering. Now, bulbs are more often than not 'naturalised' permanently into grass or mixed borders which make a lot less work. And in a small garden where you don't need a lot of bulbs to make a good display, there are plenty of unusual, if slightly more expensive, varieties where half a dozen bulbs, planted in a group, makes an eye-catching spectacle at an affordable price. Interesting bulbs to use this way include Dog's Tooth Violet, hardy Cyclamen, Fritillaria, and any of the interesting species of Narcissi, Iris, etc., and new hybrids which are always pricier than usual. Don't forget summer-flowering bulbs too, such as Nerine, Tigridia, Ornamental Onions, and Lilies.

One of the newest and most interesting uses of bulbs is as ground cover, using them to act as a carpet of spring colour over wide areas beneath trees and shrubs. This is a very useful way of adding another 'layer' of plants to a small garden, besides making a striking effect while you are waiting for trees and shrubs to take over the display in a 'low-labour' garden. It also looks very much more eye-catching than a few of the same bulbs dotted about randomly. In a small garden, low spreading bulbs like Snow-drops, miniature Narcissi, Crocus, *Anemone blanda*, Waterlily Tulips, etc. make most effective ground cover. Large Narcissi and tall Tulips may look okay when they are flowering but once they are over you have weeks of uninteresting and untidy foliage on view, which you can't clear away without adversely affecting the next year's flowering. There are two useful tips to follow when planting bulbs permanently. One is, plant them deeper than usual so you don't disturb them when you hoe. And the other is to mark groups of bulbs with labels, so you know where they are after the foliage has died down and don't try to plant something else right on top of them.

UNUSUAL BULBS FOR GROUPING

ALLIUM (Ornamental Onions) – *giganteum*, large perfectly spheri-cal heads of deep purple 3–6 ins (7.5–15 cm) across in July on stems up to 4 ft (1.2 m) tall; *bulgaricum*, extraordinarily striking, greenish heads of drooping bell-shaped flowers on 3 ft (90 cm) tall stems in June; *albopilosum (christophii)* has huge, loose, mauve heads of star-like flowers forming a large ball 8 ins (20 cm) across on 1 ft (30 cm) stems, flowers in June; *karataviense* has similar flowers in May but also broad, red-mottled leaves that curl round the base of the stems. The taller varieties look good grouped between shrubs.

CYCLAMEN – hardy outdoor types produce flowers like very frail miniature versions of the popular houseplant; *coum* flowers in early spring; *neapolitanum* and *europeaum* in autumn; all only 2–3 ins (50–75 mm) high. Grow in shade.

ERYTHRONIUM DENS CANIS (Dog's Tooth Violet) – very exotic flowers like a cross between Fuchsia and Cyclamen that appear between a pair of heavily mottled leaves; flower in March; 6 ins (15 cm). There is a very beautiful all-white version called *E. revolutum* 'White Beauty' (Trout Lily).

FRITILLARIA MELEAGRIS – most unusual chequerboard-patterned flowers in mauve and purple or white and cream; flowers April; 6–8 ins (15–20 cm); can also be grown in pots.

MUSCARI (Grape Hyacinth) – for a conversation piece, try *Muscari comosum* 'Plumosum', which has most un-Grape-Hyacinth-like flowers in bright pink fluffy plumes – very unusual.

NERINE (Guernsey Lily) – large exotic blooms like slightly curly lilies, in pink, red or white on 2 ft (60 cm) stalks, flowering in autumn. Plants are slightly tender in most regions; grow in large pots and 'dot' or stand on patio in summer.

ORNITHOGALUM ARABICUM – spectacular member of the Star of Bethlehem family with tall spikes of white flowers to 2 ft (60 cm) high. White 'wet-look' flowers in June; protect bulbs with a layer of peat in winter in cold areas.

TIGRIDIA PAVONIA (Tiger Flower) – very striking 'three-cornered' flowers in brilliant colours, with spotted centres; flowers mid summer; 12 ins (60 cm). Not hardy, lift and store in winter.

FITTING FLOWERS INTO THE GARDEN

Beds

In a small garden, where the aim is to make the garden as interesting as possible all the year round, it is not a very good idea to rely on beds planted only with annuals as, clearly, they will only look interesting in summer. You can, of course, replant with Wallflowers, Polyanthus or bulbs for a spring display – but it still leaves the bed colourless for part of the year. So nowadays it is usual to fit annuals in amongst other plants – trees, shrubs and herbaceous plants – in a mixed border, or even a mixed island bed. Here, groups of annuals planted in informal clumps are a very attractive way of introducing a splash of colour into a leafy border. You could use clumps of bright flowers to liven a mainly evergreen theme, or in between deciduous shrubs that flower when your annuals are not there. You can also use very short, 'plain' coloured annuals like pink or white Alyssum, or silver *Cineraria maritima* as ground cover to make a one-colour carpet as a background for flowering shrubs – this is often done in rose beds, for instance, as a change from bare soil. Or in a very new border where none of the shrubs have had time to grow up, you can use annuals to give a feeling of height by growing climbers such as Sweet Peas, Nasturtiums, Morning Glory or the annual variegated Hop, *Humulus japonicus* 'Variegatus' up a tripod of canes.

Containers

Annuals are probably at their very best on patios. The current 'craze' for patio planting has added a totally new dimension to bedding plants and the way they are used – now you can plan entire patio schemes based on a single colour, a special style, or simply choose plants that match the colours of your garden furniture and planters. You can also 'team up' bedding plants in hanging baskets, planters, troughs, tubs and window boxes, to make a totally co-ordinated look.

Apart from their versatility, one of the reasons annual bedding plants are so useful for patio planters is that the plants have relatively small root systems which makes them specially well suited to container growing. And the plants themselves appreciate the shelter a patio provides, which is why you'll see them growing at their best in such conditions – large-flowered varieties like Petunias, for instance, get less weather-beaten than usual when they are grown on a patio. And now that plant breeders have produced so many exciting new varieties, particularly those with dwarfer-than-usual habits, bedding plants are virtually tailor-made for container gardening.

'Dot' Plants

The idea of using 'dot' plants probably originated in very formal Victorian bedding schemes, when standard plants such as Fuchsias would have been placed at precise intervals in what would already have been a very orderly and geometrical design. Nowadays 'dot' plants can be used very successfully in all sorts of informal planting schemes, 'dotted' temporarily around the garden wherever you need a touch of colour in a shrub border, a little extra height amongst a patch of annuals, or something special in the way of contrasting foliage.

The sort of plants traditionally used as 'dot' plants are usually tender varieties such as Castor Oil Plant (*Ricinus communis*), standard Fuchsias, Pelargoniums, Canna (Indian Shot Plant), and *Eucalyptus gunnii*. But you can also use uncommon tender shrubs like *Meilanthus majus*, and Melaleuca (Honey Myrtle) and Leptospermum, or any plants which are not reliably hardy in your locality if you live in a northern or exposed area – Hebe, for instance.

Any plants used in this way can, of course, be planted properly into the garden, and dug up and potted in September, when it's time for them to go back inside. But the easiest way of dealing with them is to grow them in reasonably large pots and just 'plunge' the pot into the ground. This way the plant can be easily moved if you want a change round, and at the end of the summer can be just lifted out of the ground and moved back inside – without any damage to its roots. That's how 'dot' plants are normally used. But you can also use the same technique to make it possible to grow plants that don't like your soil conditions. If you have heavy clay soil, you probably won't be able to grow a lot of the nicer silver-leaved plants and herbs, as they are likely to rot during the winter if their roots are kept too wet. But by growing them in pots, you can 'dot' them where you want in summer, and move them to a cold frame or cold greenhouse where they can be kept on staging, out of cold, wet soil. It doesn't take long, and it works very well.

Rockeries

Although there have been no amazingly new developments taking place in the world of rock plants, there is no doubt about it – rock plants and alpines are amongst the most useful of flowers for small gardens. They are neat and compact, you can have a lot of different types in a small space without overcrowding them, and a good collection will always have something interesting going on to keep you watching. Few modern gardeners have the

Mixed border based on shrubs.

space or the depth of pocket for a traditional rockery, but in most small gardens there may be a pond, which looks superb backed by a small rock garden perhaps with a stream or waterfall running down it, or a low retaining wall or raised bed next to a patio – all of which make ideal places for rock plants.

Rock plants are also excellent subjects for growing in containers, especially the sort that re-create the alpine atmosphere, such as old stone sinks, or modern reconstituted stone troughs and tubs. The choicer sorts of alpines are also very collectable, grown in pots in a cold frame. They can be made to look more of a 'show' if you raise the cold frame up on dwarf brick walls and fill the base with gravel; sink the pots into that, surround the plants with a thin layer of granite chippings, and you'll have a lovely display.

Wild Gardening

One of the newest ideas in flower gardening is to incorporate native wild species to make a 'wild' garden. This is not just a garden left to go wild, but a carefully planned and cultivated scheme using wild flowers in a naturalistic setting. And though it may sound like the sort of thing you need a large garden to try, it's not difficult to find all sorts of odd spots where a few wild flowers fit into a small garden. They can transform a piece of spare ground behind a shed, a section of wall on an outbuilding or even just a patch of grass under an old tree, turning it into a miniature rural retreat.

A SELECTION OF THE MORE ORNAMENTAL WILD FLOWERS TO GROW FROM SEED
(Treat them just as you would hardy annuals; either sow in trays or a spare row in the vegetable garden and transplant, or sow direct into weed-free soil where you want them to flower – some varieties are best sown in autumn as they need a period of cold before the seed will germinate. NB: you can also mix wild flower seeds with grass seed and sow a small patch of wild flower lawn; ideal for a bit of wasteland behind a shed, for instance – this should only be cut once or twice a year, in early spring and late autumn).
P = perennial, A = annual, BI = biennial.

BIRD'S FOOT TREFOIL (*Lotus corniculatus*) – P, 3–4 ins (75–100 mm), sunny dryish grassy patch, yellow flowers mid-late summer.

COWSLIP (*Primula veris*) – P, 9 ins (22 cm), grassy patches on chalky/clay soil, clusters of yellow Primrose-like flowers on short stalks in spring.

ELECAMPANE (*Inula helenium*) – P, 5 ft (1.5 m), huge yellow Sunflower type flowers mid summer.

HEARTSEASE (*Viola tricolor*) – A, 2 ins (50 mm), grassy patches, mauve and yellow miniature Pansy flowers all summer.

IVY-LEAVED TOADFLAX (*Cymbalaria muralis*) – P, small trailing plant with tiny violet and yellow flowers summer.

LADY'S SMOCK (*Cardamine pratensis*) – P, 1 ft (30 cm), moist soil, lilac flowers spring.

OX-EYE DAISY (*Leucanthemum vulgare*) – P, 18 ins (45 cm), grassy patches, large white Daisy flowers mid summer.

PRIMROSE (*Primula vulgaris*) – P, 6 ins (15 cm), moist shady spot, yellow flowers early spring.

PURPLE LOOSESTRIFE (*Lythrum salicaria*) – P, 5–6 ft (1.5–1.8 m), damp soil anywhere reasonably sunny, tall spikes of purple flowers mid summer.

TEASEL (*Dispacus fullonum*) – BI, 3–4 ft (90–120 cm), any reasonably sunny spot, mauve flowers mid summer followed by large dried seed heads.

TOADFLAX (*Linaria vulgaris*) – P, 1 ft (30 cm), yellow/gold flowers like very compact miniature Snapdragons, late summer-autumn.

TUFTED VETCH (*Vicia cracca*) – P, climber, scrambles up through other plants or wire-netting, any reasonably sunny spot, long trusses of blue flowers mid summer.

VALERIAN (*Valeriana officinalis*) – P, 3–4 ft (90–120 cm), moist soil though often grows in old walls, spikes of pink flowers mid summer.

VIOLET (*Viola odorata*) – P, 2–3 ins (50–75 mm), moist shady spot, violet flowers spring.

WATER AVENS (*Geum rivale*) – P, 9 ins (22 cm), moist shade, pink/cream bell-shaped flowers mid summer.

WILD CLARY (*Salvia hormonoides*) – P, 2 ft (60 cm), dryish soil, mauve flowers early-mid summer.

WILD STRAWBERRY (*Fragaria vesca*) – P, 3–4 ins (75–100 mm), moist shade, like tiny non-runnering strawberry plants with white flowers spring, red edible fruit summer.

FOURTH DIMENSIONAL FLOWERS

In a small garden, flowers that add an extra dimension of interest to the planting scheme, such as scent, movement, or sound, are specially worthwhile. These may be plants with scented flowers or foliage; plants with tall stems that sway in a breeze, or various kinds that attract butterflies, birds or bees into the garden. Plants that can be used for decoration indoors as well as out are another good way of getting the most from your garden.

To be most effective, scented flowers need to be placed close to the house where you can best appreciate them – Hyacinths grown in pots in a porch, windowboxes or next to a front door will be noticed much more than if they were down the garden. Night-scented Stocks, which don't have very striking flowers, are best planted near a window that is likely to be left open on a summer's evening. Plants with scented leaves, such as scented leaved Geraniums or creeping Thymes, need to be bruised slightly for their scent to be released. So the best way of planting these is in tubs on a patio, or in cracks in a path or anywhere they will be regularly brushed past so their fragrances can be appreciated.

Plants that create movement in gardens are generally those with tall stems like Bamboos, flowering Grasses, ornamental Reeds and Sedges, and Miscanthus, a hardy sugar-cane-like plant. The natural environment for this type of plant is a waterside, and by reflecting the plant's movement in water you get double the effect – this is one reason why ponds, even small ones, make specially interesting features in small gardens. Another is that they, and the plant-life associated with them, help attract wildlife such as butterflies, dragonflies, bees and birds, which are themselves an extra source of interest in a small garden. The colour and movement of butterflies and the droning of bees working the flowers are garden attractions you should not be without – even in the middle of a busy estate.

Finally, plants for cutting for indoors can be blended into your planting scheme along with other annuals, herbaceous and shrubby plants. By cutting 'little and often' you give plants the change to replace what you've removed, without leaving big gaps in the garden – much better than finding room for a special 'cutting garden' in the vegetable plot!

Scented Plants

Scented plants can usually be included in with other kinds of plants in most planting schemes. Sadly, many modern strains of what were once heavily scented flowers have now lost their scent. So if you particularly want scent, choose old-fashioned varieties from specialist seed firms, or choose those varieties specifically described as well scented in 'normal' seed catalogues.

ALYSSUM 'Sweet White', 'Oriental Night', 'Rosie O'Day' – scented flowers.
ANTHEMIS CUPANIATA (Golden Marguerite) – scented leaves.
ANTHEMIS NOBILIS (Chamomile) – scented leaves.
DIANTHUS × ALLWOODII (Pinks) – scented flowers.
HESPERIS MATRONALIS (Sweet Rocket) – scented flowers.
LAVENDULUS SPECIES – scented flowers.
MALCOLMIA MARITIMA (Virginia Stock) – scented flowers.
MATTHIOLA BICORNIS (Night-scented Stock) – scented flowers.
NEPETA MUSSINII (Catmint) – scented leaves.
NICOTIANA AFFINIS (Tobacco Plant) – scented flowers, choose old-fashioned varieties.
PELARGONIUMS (scented-leaved varieties) – scented leaves.
RESEDA ODORATA (Mignonette) – scented flowers.
ROSEMARINUS (Rosemary) – scented leaves.
STOCKS – scented flowers.
SWEET PEA ('Painted Lady', 'Fragrant Beauty', 'Antique Fantasy Mixed', (old-fashioned varieties still available) 'Wiltshire Ripple', 'Lillie Langtry', 'Red Ensign', 'Royal Wedding', 'Snowdonia Park', 'Snoopea', 'Jet Set Mixed') – scented flowers.
THYMUS SPECIES (Thyme) – scented leaves.
WALLFLOWERS (especially 'Cloth of Gold', 'Blood Red') – scented flowers.

Plants to Attract Butterflies and Bees

(NB: the plants selected produce nectar on which bees and butterflies feed, rather than being the food of caterpillars; as a general rule they are plants that tend to look most at home in herb gardens, with cottage-garden plants or in tucked-away wild corners in a family garden.)

ASCLEPIAS PHYSOCARPA (Milkweed).

BORAGO OFFICINALIS (Borage).

BUDDLEIA DAVIDII (Buddleia, butterfly bush).

CENTAUREA CYANUS (Cornflower).

DIPSACUS FULLONUM (Teasel).

HEBE SPECIES.

HELIANTHEMUM CHAMAECISTUS (Rock Rose).

HELITROPIUM PERUVIANA (Heliotrope).

HESPERIS MATRONALIS (Sweet Rocket).

HYSSOPUS OFFICINALE (Hyssop).

LAVENDULA SPECIES (Lavender).

LUNARIA (Honesty).

MALVA SPECIES (Mallow).

MELLISA OFFICINALIS (Lemon Balm).

MONARDA DIDYMA AND CITRIODORA (Bergamot).

NEPETA SPECIES (Catnip).

OCIMUM BASILICUM (Basil).

ORIGANUM SPECIES (Marjoram).

RESEDA ODORATA (Mignonette).

ROSEMARINUS OFFICINALIS (Rosemary).

SAPONARIA OFFICINALIS (Soapwort).

SCABIOSA SPECIES (Scabious).

SEDUM SPECTABILE.

SILYBUM MARIANUM (Milk Thistle).

SYMPHYTUM OFFICINALE (Comfrey).

THYMUS SPECIES (Thyme).

VALERIANA OFFICINALIS (Valerian).

Plants to Attract Birds

(Allow plants to run to seed after flowering and leave stems standing to dry naturally – birds will feed when seeds are ripe, normally in late autumn and winter.)

ANETHUM GRAVEOLENS (Dill).

ECHINOPS RITRO (Globe Thistle).

FOENICULUM VULGARE (Fennel).

HELIANTHUS ANNUUS (Sunflower).

INULA HELENIUM (Elecampane).

93

Flowers for Indoor and Outdoor Decoration

If you really want good value for space, then try growing flowers with more than one use – those that can be cut for arranging in a vase, dried for winter decoration or made into pot-pourri as well as for garden use. Suitable flowers include annual, herbaceous, bulbs and shrubby species. When cutting annual flowers, aim to thin out the stems rather than strip plants entirely, and you won't spoil the display in the garden. When cutting shrubs or roses, cut with secateurs just above a leaf joint – a new shoot will soon grow from this point to replace the flower you have cut. And to make fresh flowers last longest, take a bucket of water down the garden with you and put them straight into it as soon as you cut them. Then leave them standing in deep, tepid water for 12 hours before arranging them. Add cut flower feed to the water in your vase, and they'll last very well indeed.

Everlasting flowers, for drying, should be cut when the flowers have just opened fully, and hung upside down out of direct sun in a cool, airy place to dry.

Flowers for pot-pourri should be dried in shallow layers in much the same conditions, being stirred occasionally to ensure they are all equally dried before adding ground orris root as a preservative, blending a suitable mixture of flowers together and storing the finished pot-pourri in screw-top jars until needed.

The following are some of the most useful flowers for arrangers:

ACHILLEA – the yellow-flowered *filipendula* 'Cloth of Gold' types are all very good both cut or dried; newer and rather more compact are the 'Galaxy Hybrids' in lovely colours – pink, red, salmon, yellow, etc. *Ptarmica* 'Ballerina' has double, white, button-like flowers which are also good for using fresh or drying.

ALCHEMILLA MOLLIS – large roundish leaves made up of several smaller leaflets, with loose sprays of foamy yellowy-green flowers – use fresh.

ALLIUM – round heads of pink, blue or mauve flowers on straight stems; *A.giganteum* is the largest and most spectacular – use fresh or dried.

ALSTROEMERIA – 'Ligtu hybrids' are most normally seen and make good cut flowers; *pulchra* has similar flowers but is more compact at 2 ft (60 cm) – use fresh.

94

ANAPHALIS TRIPLINERVIS – silver-grey plants with fluffy, pearl-like white flowers, good for drying.

ANTIRRHINUMS – rarely used here as cut flowers but on the Continent much favoured; double varieties specially interesting as cut flowers. Use fresh.

ASTER – best for cutting are 'Ostrich Plume' and 'Giant Quadrille' which has 6 in (15 cm) blooms. Use fresh.

ATRIPLEX HORTENSIS CUPREATA and 'Green Spire' – striking tall annuals with bright red or green spires of foliage and plume-like flowers.

CALENDULA – use any varieties fresh; taller varieties will have longer stems more suited to big arrangements, but dwarfs can still make good cut flowers.

CANDYTUFT 'Giant Hyacinth' – unusual annual variety with 1 ft (30 cm) tall, white, Hyacinth-like spikes of flower; use fresh.

CHRYSANTHEMUMS – all sorts with long stems, including annual varieties, hardy and half-hardy perennials that can be grown from seed and will flower in an outdoor border including *C. maximum* (Shasta Daisy), and exotic 'spider and spoon' types. Use fresh.

CROCOSMIA – any varieties, use fresh.

DAHLIAS – use any varieties fresh, but beware of earwigs hiding in the petals.

DELPHINIUMS – any, including new dwarf varieties if you do not need long stems. Use fresh.

DIANTHUS (Pinks are probably the best of the outdoor types as cut flowers) – use fresh, petals of scented varieties are good dried for pot-pourri.

ERYNGIUM (Sea Holly) – with heads of metallic blues and greys; good for drying.

EUCALYPTUS – foliage is very useful in fresh arrangements.

EUPHORBIA WULFENII – large heads of yellowy green flowers; use fresh but singe cut ends of stems first to prevent sap bleeding out.

GODETIA – use fresh.

GRASSES – many species including annuals and perennials producing fascinatingly shaped heads used for drying: Foxtail Grass, Feather Grass, Bowles Golden Grass, Quaking Grass, etc.

HELICHRYSUM – very popular everlasting; 'Bright Bikini' and 'Dwarf Bikini' the most compact, 15 ins (37.5 cm); taller-stemmed varieties also available.

HONESTY – seedheads are clusters of large papery discs; use dried.

HOSTA – invaluable source of foliage for flower arrangers; use fresh.

ICELAND POPPY – 'Oregon Rainbow' makes unusual and interesting fresh cut flowers.

KNIPHOFIA – any varieties tall or dwarf; use fresh.

LARKSPUR – annual Delphinium, but with shorter stems and bigger colour range; use fresh.

LAVENDER – use fresh, dried or in pot-pourri.

LIATRIS – tall, upright spikes of lavender, mauve or white, use fresh.

NICOTIANA – various colours, lime green a favourite with flower arrangers. Use fresh.

PELARGONIUM – use leaves of scented-leaf varieties dried in pot-pourri; flowers of zonal bedding Geraniums can be used as cut flowers.

PHORMIUM (New Zealand Flax) – hardy shrubs with long, broad, pointed leaves ideal for cut foliage. Use fresh.

POPPY – most species have attractive seed pods for drying after flowers are over; 'Giant Podded' strain sold specially for this purpose.

ROSES – Hybrid Teas, Floribundas, and old-fashioned roses all good for cutting; use scented varieties to dry for pot-pourri.

RUDBECKIA – annual and perennial species have large orange daisy-like flowers; 'Marmalade' a favourite for cutting. Use fresh.

SCABIOUS – large, frilly, single flowers in blue, mauve or white, 'Clive Greaves' popular for cutting though any are suitable; use fresh.

96

STATICE – use fresh or dry as 'everlasting'; available in mixed or separate colours.

STOCK – beautifully scented as well as useful shape for arranging, upright spikes of flower in various colours. Use fresh.

SWEET PEAS – one of the best flowers for cutting, and quickly replaced – the more you pick the more you get!

SWEET WILLIAM – any varieties; use fresh.

ZINNIA – tall stemmed sorts all good as fresh cut flowers; double green variety 'Envy' specially valued by arrangers.

Chapter 5

Designing the Small Garden

So much for the different ingredients – shrubs, flowers, fruit and vegetables – that go to make up a garden. But it is how you put them together that gives the garden its character. And in a small garden the way you plan the layout has a very big effect on the total productivity of the plot; not just in terms of the crops you can harvest from it, but also its more intangible qualities – relaxation, enjoyment and leisure – which are every bit as important.

When it comes to garden design, you'll find a very different set of problems in a small space to those large gardens have to contend with.

Traditionally a large garden is laid out as a series of borders around a lawn, with perhaps the odd specimen tree helping to create a vista. Large spreading plants are used to fill the space whilst keeping the costs down, as far as possible. In a small garden, the problem is not so much filling the space, as finding a way to fit in everything you might want to include. This is why careful planning is essential, whether you are starting a new small garden from scratch or altering an existing scheme. It is also why space-saving techniques like vertical gardening and multi-storey planting, and 'intensive' leisure facilities such as ponds and patios have become so popular. By grouping plants attractively, and incorporating suitable accessories to turn them into eye-catching features, any garden, however small, can be made interesting to look at all the year round – yet still be conspicuously different from those of its neighbours.

Garden Planning

One basic assumption people tend to make about gardens is that, once laid out, they should stay the same from then on. If you want easy gardening, there is no reason why you shouldn't plan things this way. But if you want to make a small garden more interesting, there is nothing like making a few alterations occasionally. This way, you can keep abreast of your own changing taste in plants, the latest fashions in garden styles, or cater for the changing needs of a growing family. It is also a good way of giving yourself a change of scene – the next best thing to having a totally new garden, but without the work, or the cost. And it's certainly an excellent way of really making the most of a small garden.

Re-planning an existing garden need not be a major exercise, as you can do it a bit at a time. Plants can be moved, new beds added and old ones grassed over, or new features built in as the mood moves you. It's no harder to re-design the garden than to rearrange the furniture in the house. And if you are starting from scratch, it's easier still to get precisely the garden you want!

The trick lies in having a plan to work to. That way, you can tackle the job in stages, whenever you have the time or cash to spare, but still end up with what you want instead of what just 'happens'. And planning a garden is not half as tricky as you might imagine – especially if you have only a small area to work on. It can be reduced to a few simple steps.

1. Draw a scale plan of the garden. Use squared graph paper, and any convenient scale that roughly fills the page, giving you plenty of room to work. Use an indelible pen for this part of the plan.
2. Mark in the fixed boundaries (hedges, fences, etc.), the house, and any other immovable features such as concrete paths, patios, tall mature trees in, or overhanging, the garden, still in indelible pen. Draw in a compass rose so you can see instantly which way faces north, south, etc.
3. Add any existing features you want to keep; specimen plants you don't want to move, beds you don't want to alter etc., again with an indelible pen.
4. Now place a sheet of tracing paper over your original plan, and trace over the permanent lines with pencil. Use this as a 'rough' plan on which to try out ideas, sketching in possible new bed shapes, positions for new specimen plants, extensions to patios etc. in very light pencil. If you like, you can draw scale models of new beds, plants or paving slabs on coloured paper, cut them out, and lay them in place on your main plan to see what they look like – this way you can easily move them round to rearrange the plan without re-drawing it.

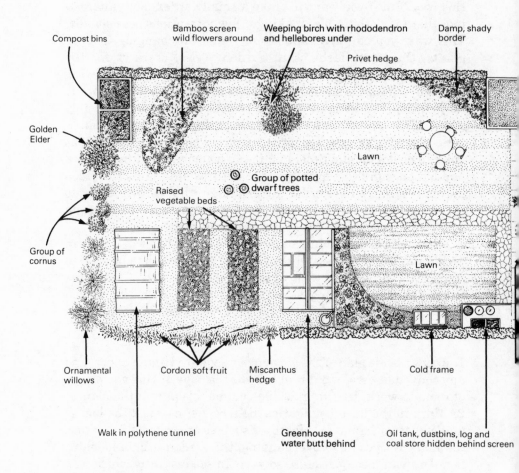

Compost bins

Bamboo screen
wild flowers around

Weeping birch with rhododendron
and hellebores under

Damp, shady
border

Privet hedge

Golden
Elder

Lawn

Raised
vegetable beds

Group of potted
dwarf trees

Group of
cornus

Lawn

Ornamental
willows

Cordon soft fruit

Miscanthus
hedge

Cold frame

Walk in polythene tunnel

Greenhouse
water butt behind

Oil tank, dustbins, log and
coal store hidden behind screen

THE GARDEN PLAN

What looks like a long narrow plot on the plan does not seem to be so 'in the flesh' because the house is situated right in the middle, dividing it into two roughly equal sized oblong gardens.

The problem:

The whole plot had been badly neglected and was full of bindweed and other perennial weeds. The back garden is completely unprotected from the north winds as the end of the back garden was completely open; the privet hedge does not extend to the end and there is nothing across the bottom of the garden.

The long straight concrete path down the centre of the back garden could not be removed. Space was needed for an oil tank, coal and log storage, dustbins, and compost bins.

100

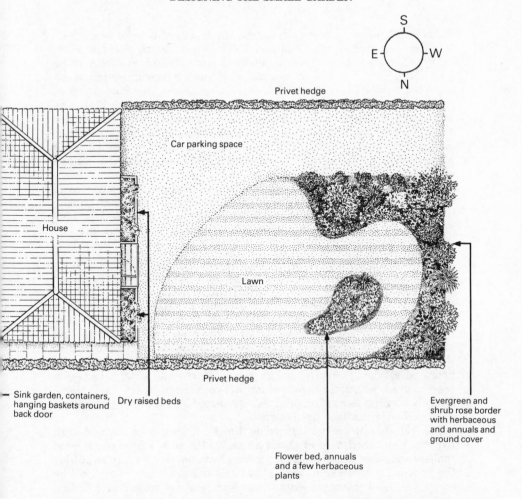

S

E — W

N

Privet hedge

Car parking space

House

Lawn

Privet hedge

— Sink garden, containers,
hanging baskets around
back door

Dry raised beds

Evergreen and
shrub rose border
with herbaceous
and annuals and
ground cover

Flower bed, annuals
and a few herbaceous
plants

The front garden, which makes up a large amount of the plot, was overlooked by the road – more privacy was needed.

Overall, more seasonal interest was wanted, with flowers to cut for the house, and plenty of fruit and vegetables – despite heavy clay soil, strong winter winds, and a high water table.

The solution:
Tackle the problem a bit at a time.

Phase 1. Sort out the mess, and begin again.

Kill grass with Tumbleweed where new beds are to go. Dig in lots of mushroom compost. Hoe out bindweed from beds or use spot weedkiller every time perennial weeds appear.

101

Phase 2. Establish framework of the garden, and provide basic amenities.

In the back garden, plant hedge of Miscanthus on north side, and wind-break of bamboo near the end, allowing room for compost bins to be concealed behind it. Use larch lap panel with clematis growing over to screen off oil tank, coal and log store and dustbins. Greenhouse, cold frame, walk-in polythene tunnel and raised vegetable beds are constructed for edible crops to give a much longer season than usual, protecting them from winter winds and wet roots. The tunnel also provides some shelter to the NE corner of the garden. The weeping birch and rhododendron makes a pleasant feature which breaks up the long narrow appearance of the back garden; it is nicely offset by the background of bamboo.

In the front garden, plant evergreens along the bed nearest the road to create an all-year-round screen giving the front of the house privacy from passing traffic. Fill in with annuals and some herbaceous plants and fast growing ground cover plants to provide a quick 'fill' and some flowers for cutting.

Phase 3. Decorating.

In the back garden, plant a low shrub border at the eastern end which provides some windbreak, but which allows something of the view beyond to be enjoyed. Groups of red stemmed cornus and golden elder will suit both soil conditions and add artistic effect. Ornamental willows such as Salix matsudana tortuosa, daphnoides and melanostachys could be added behind the plastic tunnel to provide cover for birds. The area round the bamboo and behind the plastic tunnel are planted with wild flowers to blend the end of the garden in with the surrounding countryside. The herb garden is improved by adding colourful and interesting plants with a bigger variety of uses, such as Egyptian onions, red lettuce, pot marigolds, red Basil. Damp shady border has some of original plants replaced by more interesting kinds such as Hostas, Astilbes, hardy ferns.

The old sink found abandoned in the back garden is covered with hypertufa and used to grow choice alpine plants; with a few potted dwarf conifers and other plants round it, it makes a most attractive feature outside the back door. In the front garden, annuals will gradually be replaced by 'multi-purpose' herbaceous plants, including plenty of varieties for cutting such as Astrantia. A plant group will be put in outside the front door consisting of a tall upright conifer, a low spreading conifer, a tall graceful arching grassy plant, and a few herbaceous and bulb plants – all selected to provide a long season of changing interests. Bulbs will be planted in clumps and as carpets amongst the permanent shrubs to give early and late season colour when annuals and herbaceous plants are not out. The two narrow raised beds either side of the porch offer a very sheltered, dry habitat and will be planted with choice alpines, bulbs and rock plants, choosing kinds that will not mind being in shade half the day.

Phase 4. Refining and altering.

When the back garden is more sheltered, plant shrub and herbaceous plant group to soften edge of straight path. Turn small lawn beside herb garden into patio by using a mixture of gravel, paving and prostrate herbs such as creeping thyme and chamomile. Find room for small pond. Raise cold frame and fill with gravel inside to house collection of alpine plants . . . and other alterations to be decided as the mood takes you.

102

5. When you are happy transfer the new additions still drawn to scale, to the main plan. Then set out to decide suitable plants to fill in the beds, work out how much paving you need, etc. This plan and planting scheme can then be kept in a safe place, and even if you take years to complete it, you can be sure that each time you undertake a new bit of planting you are still working to one overall effect. This saves a lot of problems wondering where to put new plants you have picked up at a garden centre – if you have a plan, you always know what you need to buy and where it's going to go. But there'll still be room for the odd impulse buy.

STYLES OF PLANTING

Drawing up a plan of the garden as it is now is the easy bit – knowing what to put in to improve it is quite another. The choice of plants, and the effects you can achieve by putting them together in different combinations, are almost unlimited. One way to cut through the tangle of possibilities is to concentrate on one particular style of garden. And the style you choose can reflect a personal interest in particular kinds of plants; it can be picked to complement the type of house you have; or to be purely practical and provide for general family leisure and relaxation. Or you might like to follow fashion and amend your garden periodically according to whether cottage gardens, 'wild' gardens, water gardens or what-have-you are currently in vogue. In a not-too-tiny garden, you could even include small 'features' of various kinds, provided they harmonise well together – for instance many gardens have a small neglected corner (perhaps behind a shed) that could be used as 'wild' area, although the rest of the garden is designed for general family use. And many kinds of garden will include a patio, regardless of the style chosen for the rest of the plot. But in each case, it takes plants with slightly different characters to create a particular mood.

Cottage Gardens

These are generally small gardens planted with old-fashioned varieties of herbaceous plants, Pinks, Roses, and aromatic plants along with perennial Wallflowers and Forget-me-nots, all grouped close together in a very natural-looking way. The lawn, if there is one, is tiny – but very often cottage gardens are completely packed with plants, leaving only space for stone or brick paths to ramble amongst them. The effect is of a garden overflowing with plants, where they spill out over the edges of paths and lawns – not all neatly lined up and tied into place. Really authentic cottage-style gardens also include fruit trees or bushes, such as apricots, apples or redcurrants, plus the more ornamentally inclined vegetables like runner beans, red-leaved beetroot, and herbs, since cottage gardens had to be useful, not just ornamental.

Town Gardens and Courtyards

It is common to find this type of garden is permanently shaded by neighbouring buildings or on heavy clay soil, besides being pocket-handkerchief sized. In these situations grass is not very practical and a much better alternative is to have a permanent hard surface instead. The garden can be paved entirely, or surfaced with a mixture of paving and gravel. And plants may be grown in raised beds, large containers, up through the gravel, or in beds between paving slabs. Unlike a patio, a courtyard or town garden is normally planted for all-year-round effect using a few very striking shaped shrubs such as Bamboos, Contorted Hazel, *Acer palmatum* varieties, and very nice containers such as the new Chinese style ones, or ornamental terracotta types. These could be planted with 'special' shrubs, or perhaps herbs or alpine plants. The key in this type of garden, which is often very small indeed, is not to overfill it. A few very interesting plants with space round them to set them off against the background looks best.

Mediterranean-style Gardens

A hot, dry 'suntrap' looks superb planted with drought-tolerant plants that suit the conditions. Plants that will do well include Yucca, Cistus, Helianthemum, Mesembryanthemum, Sedum, Senecio, Sempervivum, Eryngium, *Convolvulus cneorum*, Lavendula, Nepeta, Hebe, Osteopsermum, Othonnopsis, Perovskia, Phlomis, a lot of the herbs such as Bay, Rosemary, ornamental Sages, Rue and Thymes, and grey- or silver-leaved plants like *Salvia argentea*, Ballota, Artemesia, Helichrysum, and daisy-like flowers such as *Chrysanthemum foeniculaceum* and *Anthemis*

A well organised small vegetable garden.

Border of small shrubs backed by a rustic fence; the border has been planted on a red and pink theme. Shrubs include a pink potentilla, red hydrangea, and pink variegated Berberis thunbergii 'Rose Glow'.

(OPPOSITE) Small shrubs used as ground cover in front of taller kinds for a border where every inch of space is made good use of.

Choice small bulbs (hardy cyclamen and crocus) used to naturalise a
grassy patch in a wild corner.

(ABOVE) To break up a large expanse of continuous paving, how about using a small rock feature? Here three planted sinks have been combined with low spreading miniature conifers to create a most attractive display.

(BELOW) Paved garden with an oriental influence; note plants grown through gravel, in pots, and decorative use of pebbles.

cupaniana. To complete the picture, add a few stone paths, the occasional urn, and gravel chippings scattered over the soil between plants. Here again, you don't need a lawn – paving or gravel are best.

Family Gardens

These are the gardens where you are most likely to find a 'bit of everything' – shrubs, flowers, fruit and veg, plus a patio and a good-sized lawn for children and pets to play on. If there is room, you might even consider including a play area with swings, climbing frames, paddling pools, sand pits, tents, Wendy house and somewhere to kick a football about. It is a good idea to position a 'children's corner' in such a way that as the family grows up, it can easily be incorporated back into the ornamental garden or fruit/veg patch.

Low-maintenance Gardens

Here, the emphasis is on making a garden that looks good all the year round, but which, once it's planted, needs very little upkeep. In a really low-maintenance garden, island beds are usually chosen rather than borders round the edge of the lawn, as they are easier to work on since you can hoe from all round the edge. The most popular planting scheme for a low-labour garden is trees and shrubs (including plenty of conifers and evergreens for winter colour) inter-planted with ground-cover plants. This way, there is no annual planting, clearing and replanting to do, and very little weeding as the ground-cover plants smother out germinating weed seedlings. Techniques such as mulching, or using a residual weedkiller can cut down weeding even more, and are particularly useful in the first few years after planting while ground-cover plants are filling the space. To add greater variety to the garden without making much more work, you could plant spring and summer flowering bulbs amongst the ground-cover plants, and include a patio where annuals grown in containers provide a splash of summer colour.

Enthusiast's Garden

If you are particularly keen on one type of plant, such as alpines, conifers or trees and shrubs, it is perfectly possible to style your garden in such a way as to show off a collection to best advantage. In a small garden this can look particularly striking, and it's not uncommon to find gardens where even the lawn has been taken over, and turned into a 'walk-through' planted area, laid out with paths between well-planned groups of plants.

GARDEN FEATURES

Many large gardens are divided up to make a series of smaller 'gardens within a garden'. You'll commonly find, for instance, an area of herbaceous border, a patio, a patch of woodland, a small orchard, vegetable garden, and possibly more specialist areas such as the famous 'white' garden at Sissinghurst, a topiary garden, conservatory full of exotic plants, a herb garden, or water garden. And the same sort of thing can be done on a small scale by incorporating various features, which can be tailored to fit into even the smallest of gardens. Features such as patios, ponds, rock gardens, planted walls, and garden ornaments are what makes a small garden stand out as different from its neighbour's. And if you have a special interest, such as alpines, but don't want to turn the whole garden over to them, then many garden features provide a specialised planting environment in which such plants will thrive, and more important, look at home. Some garden features also add to the space available for growing plants, which is another useful plus in a small garden.

The key to making features look really striking, is to group together plants needing the same conditions and which associate well, preferably with other 'props' – such as stonework, an archway, pond, patio, a nice collection of containers, ornaments, or what-have-you. Even relatively unlikely objects can, by planting them appropriately, be turned into most attractive and unusual features – like old tree stumps, or decaying outbuildings. It also pays to set off your feature against a complementary background, with space round it that lets it be seen uncluttered by too much competing interest. Lawns and evergreens, walls or fences, for instance, make better backdrops for interesting features than herbaceous borders.

Water

Water is a particularly valuable feature for a garden because it contributes so much concentrated interest into a small space.

106

Water adds sparkle to the scene, and makes a garden seem brighter by reflecting sunlight. A pond also reflects the patterns made by water-side plants in its surface, which gives the illusion of a more spacious pond than you actually have. Water also introduces a new note to the garden, especially if you have a fountain or waterfall – gently running water is one of the most relaxing sounds there is.

Water features do not need to be large or complex to be effective – a half-barrel of miniature Water Lilies outside the back door will do the trick if you don't have room for anything larger. If you do have more space though, a small pond provides a wonderful opportunity to grow a fascinating range of marginal and water plants that you could not grow anywhere else in the garden, as well as somewhere to grow moisture-loving plants in a natural looking setting. Most authentic as pond-side plants are Hostas, Astilbes, Primulas, *Lobelia cardinalis*, and some of the grass-like water-side plants such as the striped Rush *Scirpus zebrina*, *Typha minima* (a miniature Bulrush), or Hakenochloa (a varie-gated gold and green grass) – these are best grown in a bog garden surrounding the pond. You can also grow all sorts of interesting plants in the pond itself, such as *Iris laevigata*, or floating Water Hyacinth (Eichhornia) and Frogbit (Hydrocharis). If you build a small rockery to one side of the pond, you could grow rock plants which, again, gives them a natural setting. And if space permits, you could create a very spectacular scheme with several different size ponds linked by waterfalls or streams, lit up at night by special underwater pool lights, forming the centre-piece of the garden.

Patio

Nowadays most family gardens include a patio. Typically this is a paved area just outside the French windows, but if the back of the house does not happen to face south or west, then it may be better to re-locate the patio somewhere else. Ideally a patio wants to be a sheltered, secluded suntrap – nice and sunny during the day, and also in the early evening which is when it will get most use. The idea of a patio is rather like an outdoor sitting room – it is somewhere you can sit in comfort even if the grass is damp, without getting your feet dirty, and where you can put garden furniture, a barbecue, sunloungers, and perhaps even a small outdoor dining table for real 'outdoor living'.

But apart from the comfort angle, it is important a patio looks the part. The most usual way of 'exterior decorating' patios is with annual bedding plants (such as Salvias, French Marigolds, Petunias, Lobelia, etc.) in pots, troughs, tubs and hanging baskets. Containers of this sort look completely 'at home' in the surrounds of a patio, and being summer flowering, are at their most colourful at precisely the time you are using the patio most. They are also very little trouble to look after, as apart from needing frequent watering, they don't want much attention. But if you want to be different, rather than going for the usual 'riot of colour' sort of patio scheme, you could opt for a fashionable 'designer' look by choosing plants of one colour scheme, perhaps shades of pink, or lilac and pink. Or, if you have a greenhouse where interesting half-hardy plants can be kept for the winter, you could grow lemon and orange trees, Oleander and Mimosa for a 'Continental holiday' look. Another alternative patio planting scheme uses hardy perennials, evergreens and conifers to provide all-year-round patio decoration. Most small shrubs, evergreens, heathers, conifers and herbaceous plants can be grown in containers. And to set them off well, why not plant a few evergreen carpeting plants such as Acaena and Thymus in the gaps between paving stones. One advantage of this sort of scheme is that you avoid the need for annual replanting. It is also a particularly nice idea if the patio is permanently on view through the living-room windows. Do remember though that even the hardiest of plants, left out in containers in winter, will need to be protected from very cold conditions. Since their roots are not protected by a surrounding layer of soil as they would be in the garden, container plants need their pots lagged with sacks or newspaper during very extreme cold, unless you can move the plants temporarily under cover.

Vertical Gardening

This is a fashionable horticultural 'buzz-word' for a technique which is very applicable to small gardens, as it simply means gardening upwards as well as outwards. And by using fences and walls, hanging baskets and multi-storey containers, arches, etc. you can indeed save lots of space, while actually increasing the area available for growing plants. But you can also use them to make a small garden look more interesting by varying the heights at which plants grow in an otherwise level site.

Suitable plants for vertical gardening are mostly climbers and trailers, but particularly those that offer the widest range of interest over the longest period of time. Especially attractive climbers for trellises, walls and arches, for instance, include *Vitis vinifera* 'Purpurea' which has purple leaves and small bunches of purple (edible) grapes in autumn; *Vitis coignettiae* which has large crinkly leaves that turn flaming orange in autumn, *Humulus lupulus* 'Variegatus', the annual variegated hop, and *Ampelopsis brevipedunculata* 'Variegata' which has small pink, green and cream variegated leaves with pink stems which are likely to die back to ground level in cold winters. Clematis are also very useful for livening up walls, as you can plant two or three different varieties chosen to flower at different times, in the same place. They look very effective climbing up through a tree or large shrub, again choosing varieties that flower at a different time to the 'host' plant. And most climbers look good trained up an old tree stump; this is a useful way of maintaining the appearance of height and maturity in a garden even when you have had to cut down a tree or shrub that has outgrown its space. Simply cut the old shrub or tree back to a framework of branches 4–6 ft (1.2–1.8 m) high, kill them by painting with diluted weedkiller (often hard cutting back will be enough without using weedkiller), and plant. Plant the climber 12–18 ins (30–45 cm) away from the trunk and train it up, holding the trails in place with string until the climber has taken a firm hold of the trunk.

For hanging baskets, what looks particularly nice is to co-ordinate the planting with nearby ground-level containers. Follow the same colour schemes, for instance, or planting styles. And where possible use plants that twine up the chains of the baskets, such as Black-eyed Susan (Thunbergia) or Morning Glory (Ipomoea), which make most effective displays as they use all the available space, instead of just half of it in the case of purely trailing plants.

Multi-storey containers, such as tower pots and strawberry planters look good planted in a style that matches other containers in their surroundings too. Both suit any plants that are naturally compact or slightly trailing in habit – herbs, other small Mediterranean-style plants, alpines, and, of course, strawberries.

Dry stone walls are another basis for 'vertical' gardening; as, by planting in the cracks between stones, you can have what amounts to a living wall of plants. But only a few plants will thrive in the dry conditions of a wall – and those that do are mostly rockplants, so choose Aubretia, Arabis, Sempervivums, Valerian, Ivy-leaved Toadflax, Iberis, Sedum, etc. for the sunny side, and plants like *Raymonda myconi*, Oxalis and small drought-proof ferns like Asplenium for the shady side. If you don't have a dry stone wall, several plants can be encouraged to root into the fragmenting brickwork of old outbuildings to 'pretty' them up – these include Valerian, Yellow Corydalis and Ivy-leaved Toadflax.

Many shallow-rooted plants such as Sempervivums, *Sedum* 'Acre' and *spathulifolium* will also grow in limited soil on top of an old wall. In a new wall, create a pocket of soil by filling a hollow space between two courses of bricks to give plants something to root into – a low, hollow-topped wall should contain enough soil to accommodate Aubretia and other trailing or short upright plants.

Herb Gardens

Herb gardens will do well in just about any dryish sunny spot; few herbs tolerate heavy, damp soil and shade. But even if you don't have suitable soil, given a sheltered sunny spot, you can grow a complete herb garden in containers. This looks particularly nice on the patio or by a back door, where the aromatic foliage and subtle shades of flowers and foliage make a pleasantly cottagey look. You can also 'park' a collection of pots on the side of some steps or along the top of a low wall if you are short of space – and still make it look nice. Or you could plant a group of herbs together in a single large container, to make more of a display – most herbs naturally associate together well, so it's not difficult to arrange them attractively. But if your soil, aspect and climate allow it, herbs can make a most attractive feature planted in the ground, especially if they are surrounded by paving, gravel, cobblestones or old brick paths, any of which set them off beautifully. Choose a tall statuesque plant for your centrepiece, such as the roughly columnar Rosemary 'Miss Jessups Upright', a clump of Dill or (if you aren't restricted to the most useful culinary herbs) Angelica, and surround it with successively shorter herbs, putting those having as far as possible contrasting shapes, textures and colours next to each other. Don't overcrowd them; let the shapes of the individual plants stand out by grouping a few plants together and giving each group its own space to grow in. You can even have paths running between the groups for a more interesting 'walk-through' garden – even if it is only in a small corner.

Wild Corners

A complete wild garden would probably be a bit too much of a good thing, although if you are an enthusiast with a country cottage it can be made to look very pretty. But even small modern-style gardens often have an odd corner – perhaps behind a shed, next to the compost heap or somewhere similar – that can be made to look much more interesting by planting it with wild flowers. They don't take much effort to look after; once sown or planted and established, wild flowers can be left pretty much alone. And because wild flowers are such a diverse group of plants, you can find something to suit just about any situation and soil type in a garden environment. Plants such as Ivy-leaved Toadflax, Valerian or Stonecrop will do well growing in cracks in walls; wild Thyme and Marjoram will also grow in cracks between paving slabs on a patio or crazy-paving path. Plenty of wild flowers thrive in rough grass – choose the sorts that grow wild in cornfield or grasslands, such as Corn Poppy, Vetches or Knapweed. And for shady spots under hedges or behind sheds, Primroses, Cowslips, Violets or Wild Strawberries make good ground cover. If you want to create a slightly more sophisticated wild look, you'll find improved versions of a lot of native wild flowers, such as double-flowered Lady's smock and Celandines (much less invasive than the 'real thing') and pink Violets in nurseries specialising in unusual plants, not to mention Bluebell bulbs in bulb catalogues and 'cultivated' Cow Parsley (*Ammi majus*) in seed catalogues.

SECRETS OF SUCCESS

The following sections offer helpful hints for planning small gardens to make the most of the space.

Lawns and Otherwise

Lawns tend to be very much taken for granted. But they are more important to the look of the garden than you might imagine – they are what sets off the rest of the garden, linking the rest of the landscape together by a common theme, in much the same way that a carpet unites the furniture in the living room. But in a very small garden, does the 'floor covering' really need to be lawn at

111

all? If you've only got a pocket handkerchief of a garden, then looking after a lawn represents a disproportionate amount of effort and gadgets for the space available – you still need a mower and somewhere to put it away, even if the mowing takes you just two minutes to do! And in town gardens lawns rarely do well if they are permanently in the shade of surrounding buildings or overhanging trees, or on inhospitable London clay.

But if a conventional lawn is not practical for whatever reason, there are alternatives – and very attractive ones, too. Paving is, of course, the obvious answer for a small town garden, and many very attractive courtyard schemes have nothing else for floor covering. But for a change – and as a way of cutting down on the cost – you could put down mainly gravel interspersed with areas of cobblestones and small groups of paving slabs, including a small seating area. This can look most attractive as you can have strategically placed clumps of plants growing up through the gravel.

Another alternative, for a sunnier spot, is to grow a herb lawn. Chamomile 'Treneague' (the non-flowering one) is the most popular kind, but you can also use Creeping Thyme, or even create a patchwork-quilt-effect by planting different varieties in informal groups, using variegated and green, flowering in different colours and at different times. These will only need clipping over with shears once or twice a year.

Or for a really 'different' kind of garden, you could go for a 'walk-through' planting scheme. Here, the idea is to fill *all* the garden with plants instead of just growing them in borders, and have paths winding in amongst them with perhaps just a small patio to sit out on. Walk-through schemes are not very often seen, but they make a delightful way to use a small garden to the full. If you are a collector you can lay the whole garden out with alpines, including an area of scree (a sloping patch of small stones carpeted with plants), raised beds and rock gardens, but the idea can be adapted to normal garden plants, cottage-garden plants, conifers and heathers, miniature shrubs or even annuals – virtually whatever you like. But since the paths play an important part of the scheme, it is worth trying to match them to the style of the planting. You could use normal paving stones in a modern garden with a mixed planting scheme; crazy paving or reproduction old stone slabs look better in a cottage garden or alpine garden setting, and in a rural setting with miniature shrubs, conifers, grasses and herbaceous plants, circles of tree stumps or rounded 'old worlde' paving slabs placed as stepping stones make lovely 'paths'.

Plant Associations

This is grouping plants together, but not just in any old groups, the plants must be carefully chosen to go particularly well together. A 'plant association' can be as large or small as you like – from an entire bed down to two or three well-chosen plants in a small group set in a lawn. But the important thing is that each plant contributes something to the appearance of the group – even when, on its own, the individual plant may not look specially interesting.

The key to putting together an effective group or 'plant association' lies in basic design skills. When teaming up garden plants to group together, you need to consider the same factors as you would when interior decorating or choosing a matching wardrobe – shapes, sizes, colours, textures. But with garden plants you also need to take into account seasonal features such as autumn colour, flowering season, evergreen or deciduous leaves, etc. as this all helps you plan how plants interrelate together. And from a purely practical point of view, you would also consider the growing environment – soil type, aspect, climate, etc. – and which plants are suited to it.

In setting about planning a group of plants, there are two ways of going about it. One is to plan out the shapes, sizes, colours, interesting features such as large colourful flowers, you want and then put names to them later. This is no doubt the logical way of doing it, but what usually happens is that you buy a plant on impulse when visiting a nursery or garden centre, decide where to plant it, and then later on pick a few other things to complement it.

Unfortunately there are no hard and fast rules for putting together a plant association that 'works'. But as a rough guide, try to choose plants with contrasting foliage textures (large, medium or small leaves, palmate, oval or small and space-filling shapes, rough or glossy surface, etc.), forms (shapes, referring to the overall shape of the plant – spire, sphere, bushy, low-spreading, prostrate, etc.), and either contrasting colours, or shades of the same colour (this can look particularly effective and is quite fashionable now). It also helps if the group has some feature in common that helps to provide a natural link between them – for instance: plants that originally come from similar habitats instinctively look right together; plants that naturally grow on acid soils automatically look good together – Heathers, conifers, Rhododendrons, Camellias, and Silver Birches; as do plants from hot dry sunny regions; grey and blue/grey foliaged plants such as Artemis, *Salvia argentea*, *Meilanthus major* and Anthemis; slightly succulent plants like Senecio, Sedum and Sempervivum, plus things like Yucca, Phormium, Romneya, Eucalyptus, Eryngium (Sea Holly), ornamental Sages, herbs and other aromatic plants including Rosemary, Rue, etc.; the moisture-lovers including Primulas, Ferns, Solomon's Seal, Hostas, Astilbes, Swamp Cypress, and Rheum (ornamental rhubarb) or the giant-leaved Gunnera. Then there are the alpine plants – miniature conifers, small species of mountain wild flowers and improved varieties of them covering thousands of different kinds; and herbaceous plants – these planted as the backbone of the garden, with grasses and a background of conifers or evergreen and deciduous shrubs, can look superb. You can find plenty more natural plant associations amongst wild flowers, cottage-garden plants, etc.

But as well as these large natural groups of plants that look good together, you also find small groups of particular plants that complement each other perfectly and make small, specially fascinating groups within a larger scheme. For instance, the unusual black-leaved plant *Ophiopogon planiscapus nigrescens* makes a fascinating group planted with blue-leaved *Hosta sieboldii* or a blue-leaved conifer, or the green and black flowered *Iris tuberosa*. Or a group of Birch trees with a Rhododendron or Pieris planted beneath them. What is so nice about these small-scale plant associations is that you can have a lot of fun discovering them for yourself. You might spot them, already 'tried and tested', when visiting a garden – Beth Chatto's at Elmstead Market, Sissinghurst in Kent, and Bressingham Gardens in Norfolk, are all particularly good gardens to visit where you'll see striking examples of plants that go well together. You can also experiment with your own, just by standing different selections of plants together when you are deciding what to buy in a garden centre.

Multi-storey Planting

This is another good way of making the most of a small plot, as by gardening on every available storey you can really pack in a lot of plants without them looking crowded, yet using all the space to the full. To see how your garden scores for multi-storey interest, imagine dividing it up into several quite distinct 'layers' of planting. In the basement, for instance, go the bulbs. The ground floor is occupied by ground-cover plants, bedding or herbaceous plants. In the first floor go shrubs, and in the penthouse, trees. Ideally, when one layer of planting is past its best, another one above or below it will be ready to take over the display and keep the interest going as long as possible. In fact, multi-storey planting automatically helps to extend the season when the garden is looking its best, by giving you more room to grow plants with seasonal interest – such as spring- and autumn-flowering bulbs, ground-cover plants with autumn tints, evergreen foliage or colourful berries, as well as the more plentiful summer flowers.

In a mixed border, multi-storey planting is quite easy to plan; it almost happens naturally as this sort of planting normally contains a blend of small trees, shrubs, herbaceous plants and annuals. But what is often lacking are bulbs – unusual varieties can be naturalised in clumps, whilst inexpensive commoner types can be mass-planted as 'carpets'. More can often be made of shade-tolerant ground-covering plants, too. These are ideal for 'filling in' beneath trees and shrubs; *Brunnera macrophylla* (the perennial Forget-me-not), Ajuga, Hosta and Epimedium all make attractive plants for such situations – in a sunnier spot the herbaceous *Clematis integrifolia* 'Hendersonii' or the prostrate Rose 'Nozomi' are ideal for ground cover with a difference. And flowering climbers like Clematis and Climbing Roses can be trained up into trees to extend the peak season of interest of short-lived flowers such as Lilac and Flowering Cherry.

But the sort of borders where multi-storey planting can be harder to plan are generally the more specialised ones. Amongst Roses, for instance, colourful annuals would be a distraction; a plain ground cover of low, silver-foliaged plants, like perhaps the half-hardy *Helichrysum petiolaris* or *Cineraria maritima*, or white Alyssum, are often used instead. For a more countrified garden, *Alchemilla mollis* is one of the best-looking ground covers for a Rose bed, though Gypsophila is also a good match. And again, a carpet of small spring-flowering bulbs provide out of season interest before the Roses start flowering. In a cottage garden, ground cover is provided by the density of plants packed into every bit of space available so there is not really room for ground-cover plants in the usual sense, but spring bulbs such as Tulips will look good planted with Wallflowers for a spring display before the bulk of the herbaceous plants come through. In a predominantly acid garden whose backbone is provided by conifers and evergreen shrubs, or Rhododendrons and Azaleas with trees such as Birches, good ground-cover plants include Heathers, the low evergreen *Gaultheria procumbens* which has red berries in winter, and cranberries or blueberries – again with spring and autumn bulbs naturalised in clumps amongst the more permanent plants. In a shady woodland garden or semi-wild corner, Bluebells, Wood Anemone, cultivated forms of Celandine such as the double 'Flora Plena' and the bronze-leaved 'Brazen Hussey', or violets make a good bottom tier, besides providing spring colour. And even in alpine and rock gardens you can introduce the multi-storey element by including a few taller, upright-growing and pyramidal conifers for height, plus ultra-prostrate growing plants like *Raoulia australis* or *Thymus serphyllum* 'Coccineus Minor' as a contrast to the usual 4–8 in (10–20 cm) tall plants.

All-year-round Interest

Although this is a subject that has cropped up several times already, it is worth exploring more fully, because it's essential to make the most of the whole growing season if you really want to exploit a small plot to the full.

And the best way to do this is not simply by planting evergreens everywhere, which would give you a garden that looked very much the same all year round, but instead by including plants that highlight the changing seasons. Every week you should be able to look out of your window and see something different. That way the garden will always be interesting, and always make you look forward to what's just round the corner – so plan your display to include as many as possible of the following seasonal highlights.

EARLY SPRING
Plants that flower on bare stems, such as Winter Jasmine (*Jasminum nudiflorum*), Winter Sweet (*Chimonanthus*), Witch Hazel (*Hamamellis mollis*), *Viburnum fragrans*, or have Catkins such as *Garry elliptica* and *Salix melanostachys*.

SPRING
Flowering bulbs, especially small varieties for using in drifts or

as carpets, such as *Anemone blanda*, Grape Hyacinth, Snowdrops, Miniature Narcissi, Winter Aconite, Bluebells, hardy Cyclamen; larger-growing kinds, including less usual sorts, for naturalising in borders in clumps such as Dog's Tooth Violet, Fritillaria, Leucojum (Snowflake); those for naturalising in colonies in the lawn like Narcissi and Snowdrops.

SUMMER
Annual bedding plants are especially valuable in the summer garden as they cover a relatively long season, but en masse they can make a garden seem rather unchanging over the June to mid-September period. So use them in mixed borders with other plants such as shrubs and herbaceous plants that have shorter flowering seasons, and choose a mixture of varieties that provide an ever-changing display over the season.

AUTUMN
Autumn-tinted foliage, especially of shrubby plants such as *Acer palmatum* 'Dissectum' and 'Ozakazuki', Blueberry, *Cornus florida rubra*, *C. kousa chinensis*, *Cotoneaster horizontalis*, Hamamellis, deciduous Azalea, Fothergilla; climbers such as *Vitis coignetiae* and *V. vinifera* 'Brandt'; and small trees including *Acer griseum*, Amelanchier, Birches, Liquidambar, *Parrotia persica*. Berries – of herbaceous plants such as *Arum italicum* 'Pictum', *Iris foetidissima*, *Actaea alba* and *rubra* (Baneberry) and shrubs like Cotoneaster, Pyracantha, Japanese Wineberry, Blueberry, Gaultheria, *Euonymus europaeus* and Red Cascade, *Pernettya mucronata* and Skimmia; fruit of Ornamental Quince (Chaenomeles), *Arbutus unedo*, the ornamental vines, *Vitis vinifera* 'Purpurea' and Brandt, rose hips (which are usually produced on species roses), and the blue metallic-looking seed pods of *Decaisnea fargesii*.

WINTER
Shrubs with coloured stems, including *Cornus alba* varieties (red) and *stolonifera* 'Flaviramea' (yellow), *Salix daphnoides* (violet) or *alba* 'Chermesina' (orange). Trees with colourful or peeling bark, including the various Birches, *Acer griseum* and *capillipes*, the Strawberry Tree (*Arbutus unedo*), and Eucalyptus. Shrubs with contorted or fastigiated stems such as *Salix matsudana* 'Tortuosa', *Corylus contorta*, *Salix sachalinense* 'Sekka'.

Adding a Fourth Dimension

However beautiful the garden you plan, there are a few 'extra somethings' that turn a merely beautiful garden into a quite unforgettable one.

One is mystery. Even in a small garden, it's a good idea to plan things so you can't see the whole garden from the back windows of the house. Much better to keep everyone guessing what may be just around the corner, by screening part of the garden from view so you have to go out and see for yourself. And even in the tiniest plot you can do this by ignoring the old advice about putting the tallest plants at the back of the border and the shortest at the front. Instead, plant groups of short plants between larger ones, where they can only be seen from certain directions. In bigger gardens, you sometimes find 'keyholes' cut into a hedge, giving a tantalising glimpse of a view beyond, and this idea can sometimes be adapted to a small scale by using screening walls or shrub borders to 'frame' a view of another part of the garden. An archway makes a nice frame for a view, too – and it doesn't have to be of your own garden, it could be the surrounding countryside, or next door's shrubbery if you like.

Scent is something else a garden should not be without. The best place to put scented plants to get the most enjoyment from them, is just by a door or window that is often opened, or where you often pass by, or brush against them. (Plants with scented leaves need to be crushed slightly before their aroma is released.)

Useful plants for scent include Hyacinths, Stocks, scented-leaved Pelargoniums, herbs such as Rosemary, Thyme and Marjoram, old-fashioned varieties of Roses, Sweet Peas, and Nicotiana (but watch out, because many of the new ones are bred without scent) and some varieties of Alyssum.

Reflections and sparkle are two very good reasons for including a pond in a garden. If you plant it with tall upright Reeds and Grass-like plants you can also enjoy the sense of movement they introduce. Ornamental Grasses can be used very effectively in other parts of the garden too, and are specially useful in a scheme made up mostly of conifers, Heathers and evergreens which needs something moving to liven it up. Another fascinating means of introducing movement to the garden is by encouraging wildlife – birds, butterflies and bees. These also add sounds to the garden; along with the tinkle of fountains or waterfalls, there is nothing more relaxing. But one of the most interesting new sensations opening up in the garden now is night lighting. This can make a remarkable difference, transforming the scene you see every day into an exotic and mysterious fairy-tale city – the perfect setting for a garden party or barbecue that goes on after dark, as well as for a little quiet contemplation when you can just sit outside late on a nice summer's evening, and enjoy what you have created.

PRACTICAL CONSIDERATIONS

But whatever else a garden is, it still has to be practical – there is always rubbish to be got rid of, equipment to be stored and laundry to be dried, even in the tiniest backyards. And these are all things that should figure in your garden plan, or you'll endlessly find fault with the finished result.

The first thing to consider is where people actually need to walk, and plan paths accordingly. Washing lines, garden sheds, back gates, the garage or vegetable garden are all places you'll need to visit regularly and if you don't put a path there, the lawn will get worn and in winter your feet will get wet and muddy. Paths don't have to be straight lines of concrete – they can be made of materials appropriate to the style of your garden, and preferably informal and gently curving, following the contours of the garden. You could use 'stepping stones'; an informally placed row of paving stones sunk into the lawn which the mower can just pass straight over. You can even buy 'temporary' paths made of a series of sections of timber that you unroll wherever you need a firm surface to push a barrow or walk without damaging the lawn surface.

So much for the essential walkways. Now for the various utilities that you can't do without, but can do a lot to conceal.

Oil tanks are difficult to hide unless you have room to actually screen them off with a section of larch lap or similar fencing – even inexpensive plant trellis will do – or you could use a block wall. Any of these take up less space than a hedge, and can be used to grow climbers such as clematis. Don't, whatever you do though, let a climber ramble straight over an oil tank, or you'll find it impossible to remove when the tank needs re-painting (which they do often or they rust and start leaking). If you are having to make an oil-tank screen anyway, make it a bit deeper and you can also use the space to store dustbins, logs, coal, bags of compost or peat, etc. as well, some of which can be slid under the tank.

A similar sort of screen can be used to hide compost bins (these take up less room than compost heaps in a small garden as the latter are inclined to spread, and you'll normally need two, one composting and one being filled). Alternatively you can screen them off with plants, such as a drift of Bamboos or an evergreen border.

Bonfire sites are particularly difficult to plan for in a small garden as they need so much empty space around them to prevent plants being scorched by wayward flames; the problem gets worse the less restricted your bonfire, so the answer is to use a proper bonfire container.

In a small garden, you are unlikely to need more tools and equipment than will fit comfortably on a couple of racks on the garage wall, but garden furniture needs space to store it in winter unless you can suspend the frames inside the garage roof and store the cushions in a spare bedroom, as many people do. The alternative is to buy the sort of garden furniture than can safely be left out all the year round – preserved timber benches, plastic or cast aluminium, and just store the cushions away indoors when they are not in use.

The odds are you will also have at least one manhole cover in the garden – usually where it will be as obtrusive as possible. The only thing to do here, since you need to leave them clear for access, is to grow a low spreading conifer such as *Juniperus media* 'Pfitzeriana aurea' alongside so its wide-sweeping branches grow over the top – or simply stand a container with a suitably spreading plant arrangement on top of it.

Your own eyesores, of course, can quite easily be hidden – but other people's may be less easy to do something about. The only thing to do here is plan your garden so that your taller evergreen plants are arranged, not only to frame your own garden, but to screen out surrounding blots on the landscape!

Stoney surroundings suit rock plants superbly – here sempervivums planted in an old stone pestle add colour and interest to the top of some steps.

Garden of hardy annuals sown in situ.

Chapter 6

Cutting down on the Chores

These days it is possible to have a lovely garden without spending every minute of your spare time working in it – unless you choose to. Because gardens are for leisure, and whether you prefer to spend your time cultivating plants, or relaxing and enjoying the view from your sunlounger, there are all sorts of gardening techniques and equipment to help you cut through the chores and make more time for doing what you enjoy most.

This is where power tools such as hedge trimmers, lawn mowers, strimmers, lawn edgers, electric hoes, watering systems, and techniques such as mulching come in. Chosen and used correctly, they can cut down the time spent on chores – without cutting down the standard of the work done and without turning to chemicals except as a last resort.

So let's look at the biggest back-breakers, and see how else you could tackle them.

WEEDING

There are three basic ways of tackling weeds – by hand, using power equipment, and by covering the soil with something that prevents weed seedlings coming through.

By Hand

Some people still like to hand weed, kneeling down with a trowel, as they find it relaxing or feel it produces a better job, as you not only remove the weed 'root-and-all', but also you don't even leave any remains lying about on the soil afterwards. A hoe is faster, and lets you work standing up, whilst also reaching into the centre of beds so there are no footmarks to scuff out afterwards. There are many new and fancy types of hand hoes appearing on

121

the market besides the 'old faithful' swan-necked hoes, draw hoes and Dutch hoes. If you like using one of the new hoes, don't be put off by the fact it has an unusual design – if it makes it easy for you to get the job done, that's all that matters. It's also worth looking out for the new garden tool sets that consist of various heads (rakes, hoes etc.) with separate handles. By choosing a handle the right length for your height, you'll be amazed how much easier the job becomes. But the one that works easier than most is what amounts to an electric hoe. This is actually a small cultivator on a long handle; the blades work with a scissoring action and you just push it through the soil – no need to work it backwards and forwards or chop like a normal hand hoe. The electric one chops off weed roots just below ground, and if you use it regularly you won't even need to collect up the debris afterwards; if the weeds are small enough, they just dry out and disappear within a day or so.

In the lawn, hand weeding is the natural alternative to weedkillers, provided the lawn is well fed and regularly mowed, it should not be as big a chore as all that! An old fashioned daisy grubber is ideal for getting out rosette forming weeds such as daisies and plantains. Just stab in and twist. If you have difficulty bending there is a long handled version that you operate by flicking a lever with your foot – the weed shoots up out of the ground root and all, and just needs to be picked up.

Weed Smotherers

Another very effective way of getting rid of weeds without making hard work of it, is by smothering them out. There are two ways of doing this: using other plants; or laying down a mulch of compost or some other material.

The plant method is not quite so simple as it sounds. This involves growing so-called ground-cover plants, which in fact often don't cover the ground thoroughly enough to smother out weeds reliably for several years, at least. During this time weeding is twice as difficult as usual, since you have to ferret out weeds from between a tangle of ground-cover plant stems. And if you have a persistent 'nasty' like Bindweed, the odds are you'll soon lose the struggle. Ground-cover plants can, however, work well if you clear the ground of perennial weeds first, plant reasonably close together to get a fast cover, and then apply a thick mulch of compost or bark chippings between plants as well.

Mulching is what you might call the most environmentally sound method of weed control. It improves the soil, is good for the plants, doesn't involve a lot of work, produces reasonably effective results and looks nice too. The idea is to cover the surface of the soil with a layer of organic material; in an ornamental bed use peat, chipped bark, or well-rotted garden compost or manure. To work well, the layer needs to be 2 ins (50 mm) deep. And ideally, it should be spread over reasonably weed-free ground in the spring so you get a full season's benefit from it.

The mulch works by smothering weed seeds as they germinate; it will also smother any small annual weeds that may be present when you apply it, so long as it's deep enough. Very persistent perennial weeds may come through later, but they are easily hoed off as the mulch makes a very friable, easy-to-hoe surface. And after the mulch has been down for six months or so, you'll start to find a new crop of weed seedlings beginning to grow on top of the mulch. A quick hoe will easily dispose of them, as the mulch is so much softer and looser-textured than soil (it's an especially useful technique if you garden on the sort of clay that sets like concrete in summer). But by the following spring, the mulch will need topping up, as much of it will have worked into the soil by a combination of hoeing and the action of worms. A 1 in (25 mm) layer may be sufficient then; 2 ins (50 mm) will be needed on light or 'hungry' soils. And if you use bark chippings, you may not need to top up for several years as they are so slow to decompose.

The big advantage of this sort of mulching over any other weed control method is that it is so good for the soil. It gradually increases the amount of organic matter present without you having to dig; it saves a lot of watering by helping to retain moisture in the soil beneath it (water well first if the ground is dry before mulching); and it insulates plant roots from extremes of heat and cold. It's also quicker than normal weeding! Nowadays it is becoming quite fashionable to use gravel for mulching between trees and shrubs. In this case you can prevent weeds growing up through the gravel by covering the soil with black polythene first. Perforate it at 6 ins (15 cm) intervals with a garden fork to allow rain through.

In the vegetable and fruit garden, you can also use mulching to cut down on weeding, but here you can use other materials that would not look so attractive in an ornamental garden. Straw or grass clippings can be used in a layer 4–6 ins (10–15 cm) deep. This is enough to smother out even deep seated perennial weeds

123

such as couch grass, provided you top up the layer of mulching material every time the weeds start to poke through. There are a few disadvantages with this sort of mulch though. One is it provides plenty of hiding places for slugs, so you may need to tackle that problem separately. Another is that, since the material is loose and therefore has to be used rather deeper than a mulch of compost or peat etc. to work as effectively, it is really only suitable to use after plants are well established. Until they are a reasonable size, you'll need to hoe instead. The other disadvantage is that, since grass clippings and straw are not already decomposed when you spread them, they will start to break down when in contact with the damp soil. This won't harm the plants, but it does deplete the soil of nitrogen, which is used in the rotting process. So to make up the deficit you will need to apply rather more than the usual amount of nitrogenous fertiliser to the crops during the growing season.

As an alternative, you could use black polythene for mulching. After preparing the soil as usual, unroll the polythene over the beds and plant through it – just cut crosses where the plants are to go. It is difficult to use this technique where you want to grow crops from seed, though you could just cut a long slit in the plastic. Seed potatoes can however be planted through crosses cut in the sheet, and are particularly labour-saving grown this way as there is no need to earth up the crop. The potatoes lie on the surface below the polythene and don't even need to be dug up, just collected! Perforated black plastic is best for this technique if you can get it as it allows you to water as usual – if not, perforate your own using a garden fork, or install trickle irrigation under the sheet (lay flat polythene tubing with a row of stitching up one side which is connected up to a hose and lets water seep through). Again, slugs can be troublesome if they get under the plastic. Either use slug bait under the sheet, or dig the edges of it firmly into the ground and hope that is enough to keep them out.

LAWN CARE

If weeding is the longest job in the garden, lawn mowing must be just about the second longest. This is where it pays to have the right-sized mower for the size of your garden – a narrow cutting width is fine for a very small garden with a lot of corners and edges to manoeuvre round, but given a largish run of unimpeded grass, a wider mower will greatly reduce the mowing time. You can also speed up by using a mower without a grass collection box, as you don't have to keep stopping to empty it. But if you opt for no-box mowing, it is essential to mow the grass frequently so you only have very short clippings which quickly dry out and vanish – long mowings will end up like hay, lying all over the lawn, and need raking up.

But mowing isn't the only chore that needs doing if you want a good lawn. The edges need trimming afterwards – and here a powered lawn edger is not only easier to use, it is also very much faster than doing the job with shears. For raking out Moss, or picking up lawn clippings, a powered lawn-raker makes very light work of a job that is particularly time-consuming and back-breaking. In a small garden, you can also use it, with its 'sweep' set at the highest setting, to collect up fallen leaves; in a larger garden you would need a separate leaf sweeper to cope with the volume of material.

WATERING

From the watering angle, gardens can be divided up into things that must be watered (such as greenhouse plants, pots and other containers on patios, newly planted seedlings, bedding plants and young plants until they are properly established), and those that may need watering (things like lawns and established borders that only need watering in prolonged dry spells).

The best plan is to check the 'must water' group – pots and young plants etc. – one or twice daily in summer by sticking a finger or water meter into the compost. They should be watered thoroughly whenever they start to get dry. The 'may need watering' group, lawns and borders, some people like to water as a matter of course as it keeps the garden looking fresher and greener in summer. But it is really only necessary in long, hot, dry spells, and even then there's no need to leave a sprinkler running for long to do the job properly. A hosepipe puts out, on average, 200 gallons (900 litres) of water an hour with the tap turned full on. And given a small sprinkler covering 9 sq. yards/metres, and normal loamy soil, you only need 12 minutes sprinkling about every seven days to keep that 9 sq. yards/metres of lawn adequately watered, even in the driest months – June and July. Sandy or very free-draining soils may need up to three times this amount, but overwatering is not good as it washes away plant nutrients and can lead to roots rotting.

Gadgets can be kept to a minimum. In a small garden, it shouldn't take too long to water patio containers and a greenhouse by hand, and turn on a sprinkler to water lawns and flower beds when needed in summer. But an outside tap is a great help – it saves a lot of trudging into the kitchen to fill a can with water, or passing a hose through the window to connect to a sink tap.

If you've much watering to do, a hosepipe is a great time-saver. Hoses come in various shapes and sizes – the sort that come complete with their own revolving reel are handy as you can hang them up by the tap ready for use, and there's no excuse for not tidying them away afterwards. There's also a 'layflat' hose that rolls up into a small, neat cassette – even better where space is at a premium. Then there are all sorts of useful 'hose-end' accessories you can get, too – car-wash brushes that fit on the end of the hose complete with special slot-in shampoo sticks; adjustable nozzles that let you spray delicate seedlings one minute and give established plants a good soaking or clean the windows the next; and hose-end fertiliser dilutors so you can feed at the same time as you water, to name but a few.

If you want to be free to go away for a few days without asking someone to do your watering for you, semi-automatic systems may be the answer. The simplest 'do-it-yourself' watering is done by standing pots on damp capillary matting (thick felty material sold for use on greenhouse benches). This can be kept moist by dangling the ends of the matting into a bucket of water. Large individual pots can be kept watered by suspending a 'wick' from the bucket straight into their pot. Given a good watering before you go, this should be enough to keep plants damp for two or three days.

Some of the simpler greenhouse-watering systems work on the same principle. Here, you buy a large plastic-bag-like container that is filled with water and hung up, which waters capillary matting on the greenhouse benches by means of a slowly dripping tube. There are also more sophisticated systems that use a rigid plastic header tank instead of a bag, and this may be refilled straight from the mains using a hose or fixed plumbing, which makes it easier still to use.

Outdoor watering, too, can be automated. Nowadays several manufacturers sell water controllers that fit to the tap, at the point where the hosepipe connects, and which turn off the water supply to your sprinkler after a pre-set time. Some can be set for several days or even longer in advance, and will turn a sprinkler

126

on and off as you wish. Sprinklers come in various types, rotating and oscillating being the commonest. (The oscillating sort are probably best for small gardens as they cover an oblong-shaped area which, with luck and good water pressure, may be the same size as the whole garden to be watered.) If you don't want a sprinkler, you can have a length of perforated hose-pipe instead, this lies round the curve of a flower bed, or snakes through a vegetable plot, and produces a gentle shower of water all along its length. And if you hate the sight of hoses and sprinklers littering up the lawn, you can install your own pop-up sprinkler system, like the ones they use on golf courses, where all the 'water-works' are underground. Don't forget that in some areas you need a licence to use a hose.

PEST AND DISEASE CONTROL

Although this is a subject of which much is made in gardening circles, in practice few gardens are significantly bothered by either pests or diseases, so it is not often that you will need to do anything about them. And now that people are so much more environmentally aware, it has become distinctly undesirable to use chemicals in the garden unless absolutely necessary. Nowadays, instead of spraying routinely with pesticides to protect plants from attack, what is recommended is to treat a problem only when it actually arises, and then only with a pesticide if it cannot be eradicated effectively by any other means. (True organic gardeners would not use chemicals even then.) If you follow this approach, it is essential to be particularly vigilant, as it is vital to spray as soon as a pest or disease gets to be a nuisance, without waiting until it has got out of hand and seriously damages your plants.

You can protect plants from a lot of pests and diseases in the first place just by good growing. Using plenty of organic matter in the soil, feed plants sensibly, and maintain good garden hygiene – don't permit weeds or rubbish lying about as this can harbour pests and disease spores. You can also protect plants from pests by encouraging naturally occurring wild predators to prey upon them – hoverflies, ladybirds and lacewings whose larvae feed on aphids, and black beetles and centipedes which feed on grubs in the soil. Even if you cannot identify the various beneficial insects, you can encourage them to visit. Simply stop using chemicals anywhere in your plot and encourage your neighbours to do the same. And plant lots of nectar-rich flowers – these attract the adult flying insects to feed, they then stay to lay their eggs. Good flowers to grow include all sorts of tagetes (including french marigolds), limnanthes (poached egg plant) and buckwheat, though many kinds of brightly coloured flowers 'work' too. Birds too are useful garden pest controllers. Robins and blackbirds will feed on vast numbers of caterpillars, slugs, snails and soil grubs, while bluetits take huge quantities of aphids from fruit trees and bushes, and roses. You can help by encouraging birds to the garden by feeding them in winter; put mixed bird seed on a birdtable, and hang fat amongst fruit trees and roses specially to attract bluetits. Apart from natural predators, you can also remove particularly large infestations of pests and diseased leaves by hand. This can quite easily be combined with dead-heading flowers, and other regular routine jobs such as watering.

GARDEN FURNITURE AND BARBECUES

Before buying bulky and expensive garden seats, tables and barbecues, it's worth thinking about practical things like storage space, as it can affect your decision about which sort to buy. Most garden furniture needs to be put away during the winter, or it deteriorates. This means having a garden shed, or space in the garage for it. If you haven't, there are now large storage bins just big enough to take a few sunloungers or chairs, and these are designed to be kept in the garden – in summer they can double as a table top for barbecue food, or a place to display potted plants. Some garden furniture is, however, designed to be left out all year round – this includes treated hardwood benches and cast alumi-nium. Even so, the cushions must be put away when they are not actually in use, as they fade in sunlight, and cotton covers go mildewy if they get damp. In summer, when you are using the seats every day, it's easy to forget – one alternative is simply to leave them out, but cover them up. You can now get heavy-duty plastic covers that fit over garden furniture (they come in different shapes and sizes for tables, sunloungers, seats, and hammocks). Barbecues need putting away or covering when not in use, as they will rust.

Most of the leisure equipment used in the garden needs a little care and attention occasionally if it is going to keep in good condition. Soft covers and cushions can be dry cleaned to freshen them up if they look grubby, but small marks will normally sponge off quite easily. Cast aluminium chairs and tables can be cleaned up with a wire brush and then painted with ordinary car paint, and wooden furniture can be sanded and varnished or stained (see the manufacturer's advice). Barbecues are the biggest problem as they become heavily ingrained with grease that is impossible to remove by normal washing. Fortunately there are now special heavy-duty barbecue cleaning products available in garden centres, and these should be used regularly to prevent too much grime building up.

GARDEN TOOLS

The basic set of essential garden tools traditionally includes a spade, digging fork, hoe, rake and hand trowel for planting. But now so many more items of equipment are available, it is often useful to have a few other 'gadgets' which can often help to speed up jobs that otherwise take a long time. As a useful bonus, they often make the job very much lighter or more enjoyable to do, too.

A strimmer is one of the most indispensable, if you want to get through the garden work in a hurry. This is an electric gadget that works by using a rapidly rotating length of nylon cord to trim weeds and long grass round trees, at the foot of a wall or fence, alongside the greenhouse or vegetable beds and anywhere else it is difficult to use shears. Some models have adjustable heads so you can also use them for trimming the edge of the lawn. Electric hedge trimmers are also very much faster than doing the same job with shears.

If using electric gadgets in the garden, it is a very good idea to plug them into a circuit breaker – this cuts off the power before you are at risk of a shock if you should inadvertently cut through a cable. They are also a good safeguard if you happen to cut grass or hedges while they are wet (which isn't advisable, at the best of times).

RUBBISH DISPOSAL

This is one of the thornier areas of gardening. Most dustmen will not take garden rubbish, so you have to find other ways of getting rid of it for yourself. Soft, leafy waste such as lawn mowings, weeds, hedge clippings and prunings are best composted and returned to the garden – they provide a valuable source of bulky organic material that can very beneficially be used for mulching

129

or soil improvement generally. The traditional method of making compost in a heap often takes a year or more to do and occupies quite a lot of space in the meantime. Compost bins keep the rubbish tidy while it rots down, and are a more reliable way of producing good compost than a plain heap. Either way, you need two heaps or bins – one rotting, while the other is being filled up.

There is a knack in turning garden rubbish into good compost quickly. Instead of just piling the rubbish up any old how, put your grass clippings and weeds in alternate layers no more than about 6 ins (15 cm) deep with a bucketful of soil or a handful of compost accelerator between them. (These both provide a concentrated source of the bacteria responsible for rotting compost.) Then damp down each new layer with a hosepipe and firm it down lightly. Don't make a heap of just one kind of material – lawn clippings alone will go slimy – but instead mix grass cuttings with weeds, kitchen waste and fallen leaves. Avoid adding woody materials such as cabbage stalks and fruit tree prunings, which take longer to rot. And avoid putting roots of perennial weeds on your heap, just in case it does not heat up enough to kill them properly. With luck, this should give you usable compost in six to eight months. But if space is really short you can speed up the composting process even more by using one of the new rotating compost bins. By cranking the handle and turning the compost every few days it rots faster, so you make more compost from the space in less time.

Alternatively you can get rid of much garden rubbish by burning it, so long as you have tolerant neighbours and don't live in a smokeless zone. A proper bonfire container takes up much less room than a bonfire made by just piling up a load of rubbish and setting fire to it, as the rubbish cannot fall over or blow about. But the sort that takes up least space of all is the kind of burner that looks like a metal dustbin on legs, complete with lid. This can be stood relatively close to shrubs etc. without risk of scorching them, as the flames are contained inside the solid metal sides.

In an area where bonfires are 'out', or where you have large amounts of garden rubbish to get rid of, you need a more direct means of disposal. The answer is either to take it to the local tip (phone the council to find out its whereabouts), or hire a small builders' skip (look them up in *Yellow Pages*), which can always be shared with a neighbour to halve the cost.

Index

131